CORRUPTION
& POLITICS IN
Contemporary
M E X I C O

CORRUPTION
& POLITICS IN
Contemporary
MEXICO

STEPHEN D. MORRIS

The University of Alabama Press
Tuscaloosa • London

Copyright © 1991 by
The University of Alabama Press
Tuscaloosa, Alabama 35487–0380
All rights reserved
Manufactured in the United States of America

∞

The paper on which this book is printed meets the
minimum requirements of American National
Standard for Information Science-Permanence of
Paper for Printed Library Materials, ANSI
Z39.48-1984.

Library of Congress Cataloging-in-Publication Data

Morris, Stephen D., 1957–
    Corruption and politics in contemporary Mexico /
Stephen D. Morris.
        p.   cm.
    Includes bibliographical references (p.   ) and index.
    ISBN 0-8173-0525-4
    1. Corruption (in politics)—Mexico. 2. Mexico—
Politics and government—1970–   I. Title.
JL1229.C6M69   1991   90-47510
320.972—dc20   CIP

British Library Cataloguing-in-Publication Data available

To my friend and wife, Celina

Con dinero baila el perro . . .
sin dinero uno baila como perro.
[With money the dog dances . . .
without money one dances like a dog.]

Poderoso caballero es Don dinero
[Money is power]

Popular Mexican sayings

Contents

Tables and Figures

Tables

Figures

Preface

This book addresses the causes, effects, and dynamics of political corruption in Mexico. It springs from the assumption that systematic analysis of corruption is critical to a better understanding of the politics of Mexico; that despite the paucity of previous analyses and many conceptual and methodological obstacles, the importance of the subject matter demands its treatment. This effort should therefore be seen not as definitive but as an initial step in trying to understand this neglected aspect of Mexican politics.

Corruption, as a topic of research, invites certain misunderstandings. Corruption is a broad concept, conveying a variety of moral connotations. This inquiry into political corruption is not intended to depict the Mexican people or society as any less or more moral than others. The objective is not to expose scandals and wrongdoing by Mexican officials, name names, or point fingers; it is an academic endeavor. Scandals are discussed and examples of corruption used for illustrative purposes, but the analysis strives to be more theoretical than anecdotal. Finally, although corruption is clearly widespread in Mexico, no effort is made to compare corruption in Mexico to corruption in other countries. The study should therefore not be construed to imply that Mexico suffers more or less corruption than other countries or that corruption does not exist in my native country, the United States.

Research for this book extended over a period of years during which time I acquired many intellectual and personal debts. I wish to acknowledge the help of my colleagues at La Universidad de las Américas in Puebla, where I served as a visiting professor for the 1985–86 academic year; the many students in Puebla who participated in the public opinion survey in 1986 and others who assisted in arranging interviews with members of the elite, specifically Héctor Franco Rey and Fernando González; *mis compadres* Ernesto Alvarado Ruiz and Lucy Díaz Solórzano, who diligently assisted in the collection of corruption-related news articles; Professors Edward Muller and John Wahlke of the University of Arizona, who offered helpful comments and recommendations; my friend and colleague John T. Passe-Smith, who gave invaluable assistance; and most warmly, my mentor, Professor Edward J. Williams, who uniquely combines scholarly dedication with human compassion. I wish to acknowledge the assistance of a research grant from the University of Arizona that facilitated work on the original project. Finally, I wish to thank my children David and Tania for their patience and my wife, Celina, who assisted in every aspect of the research and constantly provided encouragement and inspiration. Like my love, this book is dedicated to her.

Initial formulations of some of the ideas elaborated here were presented in an article in *Corruption and Reform* 2, no. 1 (1987): 3–15. Permission to use statements and ideas is appreciated.

Without the help of these warm friends and colleagues there would be no final product; yet I alone am responsible for its contents, conclusions, and translations.

Introduction

The political significance of corruption frequently transcends its prominence in scholarly writings. Marginalized alongside such esoteric affairs as betrayal, secrecy, and propaganda,[1] corruption is seldom addressed in comparative texts; mainstream thought rarely incorporates it. Such asymmetry overabounds in the case of Mexico, where corruption endures as both an institutionalized component of the system and, according to the editor of one popular Mexican magazine, "Mexico's number one problem."[2]

Corruption pervades the Mexican political system. Most conspicuous at the lower levels, particularly among the police, is the *mordida* (literally "the bite"). Normally referring only to small payments to police in exchange for "overlooking" both real and often imagined traffic violations, this low-level form of corruption hardly qualifies as a petty problem or a simple, practical solution to the police's low wage. Spectacular revelations of the operations of the Mexico City police department under the leadership of Arturo Durazo Moreno (1976–82), for example, exposed an elaborate network of extortion, fraud, and kickbacks involving almost every member of one of the world's largest metropolitan police forces.[3] Until his incarceration, the earnings from this mafialike system afforded the police chief the life of a millionaire on a monthly salary of about $350.

Beyond the *mordida,* local, state, and federal judicial police have been implicated in hosts of kidnappings, robberies, thefts, drug trafficking, and other criminal activities. A group of police in 1983, for instance, was discovered operating a large auto-theft and bank-robbery ring; a report in 1985 exposed a gang of police routinely stealing the pay of industrial workers as they left the factory;[4] in 1989, the Mexico City office of the Federal Intelligence Directorate (ID) was accused of "kidnapping, extortion, robbery, torture and homicide" after more than sixty cases of abuses were received by the city's Assembly of Representatives. Following the arrest of two codirectors, the ID was disbanded, reminiscent of the breakup in 1982 of the ID's predecessor, the Directorate of Investigation for the Prevention of Delinquency (DIPD), also implicated in a variety of abusive activities.[5] Reports of police and military involvement in drug trafficking—the narco-power connection—grew common during the late 1970s and the 1980s,[6] highlighted by the investigations surrounding the murder of U.S. Drug Enforcement Agency agent Enrique Camarena in 1985 and the murder of journalist Manuel Buendía in 1986 by the director of the Federal Security Police, who was arrested in 1989. In fact, police corruption reached such sordid levels that one observer sadly concluded in 1983 that "society has come to fear the police more than it fears the criminal";[7] or, as Heberto Castillo noted in *El Universal* six years later, "the worst criminals come from the police corps."[8] Indeed, it is at times difficult to distinguish police from criminal in Mexico.

But despite their greater visibility, the police have no monopoly on corruption in Mexico. Countless cases of bribery, extortion, fraud, kickbacks, nepotism, and unexplained wealth routinely attend the upper echelons of the government pyramid. In 1976, for instance, two state governors stood accused of misusing 36 million and 400 million pesos.[9] The early 1980s unleashed a rash of public investigations and scandals centering on such once-powerful figures as the head of the huge state--

owned oil monopoly PEMEX (Mexican Petroleum), leaders of national trade unions, state governors, and even former presidents. Besides providing lucrative employment opportunities for many members of his family, for instance, it has been estimated that President José López Portillo (1976–82) skimmed from $1 to $3 billion.[10] General estimates of the sums pilfered in the major cases exposed in the early 1980s approach $20 billion, enough, according to one report, to have paid the interest on the huge Mexican debt for 1983, 1984, and the first five months of 1985.[11]

Besides its vertical omnipresence, corruption also permeates the massive Mexican bureaucracy horizontally: apparently few parts of the government have escaped the seductive enticements of corrupt gain. As Lola Romanucci-Ross categorically states: "It [corruption] exists on all levels and affects every office or formalized position."[12] Indeed, just a sprinkling of reports reveal that the Mexican customshouses are "plagued by corruption and abuse of authority";[13] that businessmen routinely pay "political middlemen" to secure through illegal means an array of operating permits and licenses;[14] that sinecures are commonplace throughout the bureaucracy; that illegal land sales are widespread; and that *sobrecitos* or payoffs from bureaucrats and politicians to journalists are standard operating procedure. Money has secured the release of criminals from prison,[15] bought college degrees, obtained lucrative government or union jobs, and even purchased elementary school examinations.

A cursory glance into the past suggests that the pervasiveness of corruption in Mexico is not a recent phenomenon. Eric Wolf acknowledges widespread corruption during Mexico's colonial epoch, associating it with the formal and informal discriminatory barriers that confronted the growing mestizo population;[16] Lucas Alemán refers to the corrupt privileges enjoyed by the Mexican military during the middle of the nineteenth century;[17] and Alan Knight and Paul J. Vanderwood highlight the common practice of "converting" bandits into police during pre- and postrevolutionary periods.[18] President Alvaro Obregón (1920–24) publicly acknowledged the tactical use of corruption: "there is no general that can resist a barrage of 50,000 pesos";[19] and President Miguel Alemán Valdés (1946–52) left a world-renowned legacy of corruption and ill-gotten gain. Frank Tannenbaum's depiction of Mexican politics in the late 1940s crystallizes the historical magnitude of corruption: "Perhaps worst of all is the *mordida*—that has grown in a widening circle from official to unofficial persons and is now perhaps the greatest single impediment both morally and politically to good government and economic progress."[20]

The ubiquity of corruption in Mexico is widely acknowledged both inside and outside the country. The countless anticorruption campaigns that dot Mexican political history attest to its widespread nature. President Luis Echeverría Alvarez (1970–76) called corruption a "cancer of the Revolution," adding that "for no one is it a secret that the police abuse [their authority]," resulting in what he referred to as "the payment of the fatal '*mordida.*'"[21] President López Portillo averred during his anticorruption drive that if famed revolutionary Emiliano Zapata were alive, he would fight against dishonest government officials.[22] His successor, President Miguel de la Madrid Hurtado (1982–88), later mobilized the anticorruption sentiment to heretofore unknown heights through a massive campaign titled "Moral Renovation." And in his initial year, President Carlos Salinas de Gortari (1988–94) fashioned a similar program, toppling from power strong labor leaders and financiers in corruption-related scandals. Yet despite all the rhetorical postures, legal reforms, prosecutions of public officials, and promises, apparently the level of corruption in Mexico has not been substantially reduced.

The antiquity, centrality, and pervasiveness of corruption in Mexico raise important questions for understanding both the nature of corruption and Mexican politics. Major theoretical queries center on the causes of this corruption and its effects. Specifically, to what extent do the unique features of the Mexican system (its revolutionary origins or one-party rule) relate to the persistence of corruption? Does corruption enhance the stability of the government or undermine popular faith in the government? Why have so many anticorruption efforts failed? How does the Mexican public feel about corruption? Have the debt crisis and economic decline of the 1980s altered the situation?

The current inquiry addresses these and other related issues. It attempts to rectify the asymmetry noted earlier by exploring this salient yet unattended dimension of the polity. By incorporating this concern for corruption, it strives to provide a more complete and comprehensive analysis of Mexican politics.

CORRUPTION
& POLITICS IN
Contemporary
MEXICO

1 A State-Society Approach to the Study of Corruption
Definition, Typology, Cause, and Consequence

The systematic study of political corruption encompasses matters of definition, typology, cause, and consequence, linked by a common theoretical framework. A substantial body of literature explores these issues, but many problems exist. The countless definitions inadequately set out the fundamental normative and behavioral dimensions of corruption and fail to incorporate the phenomenon into a broader theoretical framework or to deal accurately with the question of private interests. Typologies of corruption, though equally rife, also seem to lack clear theoretical relevance. Existing explanations of corruption can be attacked for projecting confusing and contradictory hypotheses, for being fragmentary, and for failing to differentiate various types of corrupt behavior; those centering on the functions of corruption also seem incomplete. Some, for instance, underscore the positive effects of corruption in integrating a ruling elite but fail to question whether corruption influences feelings of legitimacy toward government or inspires destabilizing protests and mobilizations.

This chapter addresses these important conceptual and theoretical concerns. Attention centers first on the issue of definition and conceptualization, setting out the normative and behavioral dimensions of corruption, and then ties these to a

1

broader model of the state. Subsequent analysis differentiates two broad patterns of corruption, extortion and bribery, followed by attention to causes and functions of corruption. The chapter concludes by projecting the application of the framework to the Mexican case.

The Concept of Corruption

The initial task in analyzing corruption centers on definition. Answering the question, What is corruption? has long proved difficult and been the subject of lively debate.[1] It has been defined variously as "the illegitimate use of public power for private gain,"[2] "all illegal or unethical use of governmental activity as a result of considerations of personal or political gain,"[3] or simply as "the arbitrary use of power."[4]

As a form of deviant political behavior, corruption is political conduct contrary to political norms. This definition underscores both its normative and behavioral components. The normative aspect of corruption centers on the valuative standards or rules that determine political propriety: the criteria used to judge the legitimacy or illegitimacy (i.e., the "corruptness") of a political act; the behavioral aspect corresponds to observable actions.

Although debate rages,[5] the normative aspect of corruption can be equated with some broad notion of the "common interest"[6] that lies at the core of the modern state's legitimacy. The norm provides the standard by which all acts of government are to be interpreted and judged. Accordingly, any private usurpation of that pertaining to the public domain which negates this principle invites condemnation.

Though the broad barriers defining corruption often appear universal, they are filtered through particular political cultures and experiences so that little agreement attends the legitimacy or illegitimacy of specific political acts. Standards determining legitimate political activity in a given society (and thus corruption) often appear vague, elusive, and, at times, illogical. This is to be expected: if determining what is or is not in the common interest of society prompts dispute, then locating its antithesis should be no less evasive. Clearly common interest is a value-laden term, and high degrees of definitional ambiguity are unavoidable.[7]

The slippery distinction between patronage and favoritism helps illustrate this ambiguity. Though the two political acts are empirically similar (e.g., the granting of a political position to a friend or acquaintance), they tend to evoke different emotional or valuative responses. Patronage normally carries fewer negative overtones than favoritism to the degree that it can be legitimately construed as serving some greater concern than the personal interest of the public official. Cabinet-level appointments (where patronage or favoritism is allowed), for instance, are thought to be qualitatively different from lower-level bureaucratic appointments for precisely this reason.

The second aspect of corruption is behavioral. Here corruption consists of a special type of political conduct characterized by individual acts by public officials and private citizens that spawn particularistic, situation-specific outcomes within a furtive environment.

First, corruption involves political behavior by individuals, often in the form of limited, face-to-face dyadic encounters, unwritten agreements, and the personal exchange of resources;[8] but may include just one actor with no reciprocal arrangement whatsoever. In the context offered here, corruption refers only to political acts (e.g., political corruption)— acts impinging on the authoritative allocation of values in society—and therefore must involve individuals acting in the name of the state. Second, corruption fashions particularistic as opposed to universal political results. This means that the immediate outcome of a corrupt act is limited to the particular situation surrounding it and does not extend out universally, creating a binding precedent for all or similar dealings with the government. Third, corrupt acts are normally cloaked in secrecy and hidden from public view because of their illegitimacy and (normally) illegality.[9] Although the existence of corruption may be common knowledge throughout Mexico, few are willing to admit to specific acts of impropriety.

A final and important issue that warrants attention concerns the role of personal gain or interest, a component of most definitions that is not included in the conceptualization here. Indeed, most definitions of corruption emphasize personal interest. Lawrence Sherman's definition is typical: "the illegal use of organizational power for *personal gain*" (emphasis added).[10]

Including personal gain or what is tantamount to private interest in a definition of corruption presents two major problems. First, it is generally held that all acts are a function of personal gain; in formal theory, this is referred to as "rationality." Consequently, *all* acts by government officials, whether corrupt or otherwise, are thought to be motivated by a rational promotion of private interest. In other words, a noncorrupt act is promoted by personal interest just as is a corrupt act. Since personal interest is an assumption of human behavior and a constant, it need not be included in a definition.

Moreover, corrupt acts do not always *exclusively* promote private concerns. As Gabriel Ben-Dor suggests, "corruption may benefit oneself, one's family, one's friends or acquaintances, an ethnic group, an institution or even a cause."[11] This distinction prompts Stanislav Andreski to distinguish between "egoistic" and "solidaristic" or group-level forms of corruption.[12] For example, nepotism and conflict of interest yield benefits to the individual public official but also promote broader family and corporate interests. Likewise, the "coerced" involvement of a police officer in a corrupt network directed by his or her superior also serves the officer's personal interests but hardly qualifies as an example of pure avaricious behavior.

Viewed from this microperspective, then, corruption involves a rational act by a public official that deviates from the ideologically sanctioned promotion of the common interest. From a broader perspective, however, it consists of an agent of the state (the public official) acting contrary to the rules of the state. In this larger sense, corruption corresponds to discord or incongruence between two dimensions of a single state. Moreover, since a corrupt act may involve organizational goals above and beyond individual gain—an intermediate level—the nature of the inconsistencies may be even greater. In pursuing this conceptualization of corruption, attention thus turns to the state and the intermediate role of organizational interest.

Corruption and the State

The state is composed of three basic components or levels: a legitimizing ideology, an organizational apparatus, and personnel. An abstraction, the legitimizing ideology is a belief system made up of the basic principles and values denoting political legitimacy. Like Gaetano Mosca's classic notion of "political formula,"[13] this ideal dimension of the state informs broad philosophical principles, ideological currents, constitutional drafts, legal statutes, and mythical codes: it provides the transcendental foundations wherein political authority resides.

The second component of the state entails structures and organizations. At this level of analysis, the state refers to "an independent group of institutions that form the apparatus in which the power and resources of political domination are concentrated."[14] This realm of the state encompasses such organizations and institutional patterns as the government, the various bureaucracies, congress, and the executive. Though these organizations have written and perhaps unwritten rules that set out their objectives, goals, and procedures, the authority they possess stems from the state's legitimizing ideology. They serve as the organizational expressions of the state.

Finally, at the lowest level of analysis, the state encompasses the personnel that occupy the various roles of the state's organizations.[15] Here, the state is personified by those acting in its name and partaking of its authority. It is here that political acts such as corruption occur because neither an ideology nor an organization can truly act.

The normative dimension of corruption that sanctions the pursuit of the common interest for public officials and differentiates between the public and the private spheres of society is a component of the state's legitimizing ideology, whereas the political act of corruption takes place at the lower level among the personnel. Corruption thus represents secular, political heresy because the acts of those imbued with the authority of the state's legitimizing ideology negate a basic principle of that ideology.

Public officials are expected to promote the common interest, but they are not expected to denounce private interest; rather, it is expected that their rational pursuit of private interest will coincide with the goals and interests of their organization (e.g., the bureaucracy), which in turn are consistent with the pursuit of the common good. Ideally, the state postures no breaches among the dictates of its legitimizing ideology, the goals of its various organizations, and the behavior of its employees; form and substance merge. But this is rarely the case; in the real world inconsistencies and gaps among the three levels of the state are often apparent.

Within this framework, then, corruption can be said to occur when the behavior of personnel is inconsistent with the state's norms. This breach can take two general forms: the behavior may be inconsistent with broader organizational norms or interests (i.e., exclusively promote the private interest of the personnel); or the behavior may be consistent with broader organizational norms or interests that are in turn inconsistent with the dictates of the state's legitimizing ideology. From this perspective, the crucial question then becomes, What factors enhance the congruence of individual persons' action to organizational interests and the congruence of organizational objectives to broader goals depicting the common interest? In other words, when do the rational acts of public officials fit the rules governing their positions? And when does a government structure promote what its personnel publicly admit to be (and the society accepts as) in the best interests of the people?

The possibility that corruption (besides promoting private interest) may also further organizational goals greatly opens up the playing field because both private organizations and public organizations impinge on behavior. According to Joel S. Migdal, all social organizations (not only those of the state) attempt to "subordinate individual inclinations to the behavior these organizations prescribe"[16] (seek a congruence between private-regarding and organizational-regarding conduct). This is accomplished by offering a mix of positive and negative, tangible and intangible sanctions. Thus in pursuing personal interest, individuals respond to the organizations offering the best opportunity for upward mobility and survival. The rational actions of personnel from the state may therefore correspond to the interests of organizations outside the state (i.e., private social organizations), which would clearly be inconsistent with the goals of the state's legitimizing ideology (and probably with the state organization from which the personnel derive their authority).

Bribery and Extortion

In that corrupt behavior may promote the exclusive interests of the individual or the organizational concerns of the state or social organizations, a typology to differentiate basic forms of corruption that fits this framework is useful. Previous typologies of corruption have accentuated a host of criteria to differentiate corrupt acts, ranging from the degree of deviance to underlying motivations.[17] Here, attention centers only on discerning two broad classes of corruption—bribery and extortion—based on the direction of political influence and the types of organizations involved.

Bribery requires a dyadic encounter between a private citizen and a public employee in which the private citizen induces a desired response on the part of the public official through the use of such positive sanctions as monetary gain. Extortion, by contrast, finds the public official either influencing the behavior of the citizen through the use of such negative sanctions as a threat further to abuse authority (in its dyadic form) or refers to autocorruption in which only the public official is involved. In both bribery and extortion, an illegitimate power is exerted but in different directions.

At the two extremes, the broad distinction between bribery and extortion is rather straightforward and conforms to popular wisdom. As used here, however, the terms are more specific. In some cases, the distinction may be impossible to make. For example, it is common in many countries for people to pay a bureaucrat to speed up an often timely and burdensome procedure: to cut through the red tape.[18] Although commonly thought of as bribery, this act may be a form of extortion if the public official purposefully constructs those bureaucratic obstacles so as to solicit the bribe.[19] Although this act may seem trivial (and one might think that what is extorted is a bribe), in the former case, bureaucratic red tape represents the root cause of the corruption, whereas in the latter case it is merely a consequence. This analytical distinction facilitates attention to this crucial causal difference.

Corruption is a rational act and therefore promotes the private interests of its participants. This is true of both bribery and extortion, yet there is some difference. Paying a thousand pesos is preferable to a traffic citation of two thousand pesos regardless of whether the traffic violation was actually committed. Extortion often differs from bribery, however, in that the relationship is somewhat more asymmetrical with greater benefits accruing to the public official because the positive sanction offered in a bribe represents a cost to the citizen, whereas the negative sanction employed in the case of extortion (abuse of authority) is not lost to the public official but can be reused within certain limits.

Other corrupt acts can be classified under these two broad categories. Graft or peculation,[20] like autocorruption, is a form of extortion; a kickback is a form of bribery, although the funds are delivered after the favor is granted rather than before; even favoritism and nepotism (the granting of political favors to friends and relatives) can be viewed by the nature of the relationship. Strong family norms, for example, usually underlie nepotistic behavior.[21]

Crucial to classifying corrupt acts as either bribery or extortion is identifying the organizational interests involved in a corrupt exchange. Thus even if a precise reading of the nature of the exchange is impossible, it is important to try to identify the organization(s) (and their interests) entangled in a corrupt exchange. If corrupt acts further the interests of a family, a political clique, or a business, for instance, then the norms, structures, and nature of these organizations constitute an important variable in the equation.

Thus far the framework depicts corruption as an incongruence between the behavior of the state's personnel and the dictates of its legitimizing ideology that may take one of three forms: the behavior may respond exclusively to private interest concerns or it may parallel the objectives of the state's or competing social organizations. The first major theoretical question thus centers on the factors that fashion these inconsistencies.

The Causes of Corruption

A variety of explanations of corruption have been offered.[22] Generally, causal theories produce an array of contradictory hypotheses, appear fragmented, and fail to differentiate various types of corrupt behavior. Even the most developed unifying framework for interpreting corruption, modernization, presents problems.

First, literature on corruption offers many contradictory hypotheses. The contention by some that centralization of authority fosters corruption, for instance, contrasts with the argument by others that decentralization feeds it.[23] Similar dispute centers on whether the lack or existence of strong political institutions facilitates corruption.[24] And some contend that the absence of legitimate access to opportunities for mobility enhances the prospects for corruption, while others argue that lack of access to political influence provides the causal key.[25]

Second, explanations often appear fragmented and disjointed, with few comprehensive efforts mounted to link the many causal factors. Specific bureaucratic structures conducive to corruption are rarely tied to broader social structural variables. How does bureaucratic centralization or professionalization, for instance, relate to the issue of access to legitimate means of influencing public policy, the problem of a lack of government supplies facing unlimited demands,[26] or the issue of government accountability,[27] all of which have been linked to corruption?

Third, existing theories fail to differentiate various forms of corruption. In most cases, theoretical arguments posit a major causal agent as producing corruption; none really specifies what type of corruption may result or what specific factors may relate to different corrupt acts. The contention by James C. Scott, that corruption springs from the systematic denial of political influence to a particular group, may significantly account for the existence of widespread bribery as the group "buys" its political influence, but provides only limited insight into the causes of extortion or nepotism. Indeed, part of the problem of fragmentation and contradictory hypotheses would appear to stem from this general failure to discriminate types of corrupt acts. Rather than contradictory, it is possible that government centralization produces one type of corruption while government decentralization promotes a different type.

A final problem relates to the theme of modernization that underlies much of the theoretical analysis on political corruption. Envisioning a transition from traditional values and institutions to modern ones marking the process of development, modernization treats corruption as the playing out of this conflict between the traditional values that condone corruption and the more modern values that condemn it. As a country develops, it is argued, its values undergo changes that lead eventually to the elimination of corruption.[28]

Critiques of the modernization approach, however, point out the many differences that separate the experiences of the developing countries of today from those of the now developed countries, downplay the causal role of values, and question whether corruption actually has disappeared in the developed world. States undergoing the process of development today indeed offer a profile distinct from those of the past: ideologically, they confront a rapid diffusion of foreign and domestic values through modern technologies that impinge directly on feelings of legitimacy and protest; structurally, they reflect a higher level of foreign political and economic influences, a weaker internal capitalist class, and a stronger state role. Such crucial historical differences effectively reduce the theoretical significance of any similarities and hence the utility of the approach. In recent years, the study of political development has fruitfully used other approaches such as dependency, corporatism, and state-society.

Critics of the modernization approach also downplay the

causal role of values. Parochial, particularistic, and ascriptive orientations that make up the pattern variables are clearly symptoms of underdevelopment but, many feel, not its cause. This point holds that values sustaining corruption may coexist with the phenomenon but may not constitute its root cause. Values may provide the inertia and make up the socialization process by which corruption is perpetuated without constituting its true cause.

Many question (perhaps considering it patronizing) the tendency of the modernization perspective to minimize the importance of corruption by assuming its disappearance as a country develops. This "apologetic" view unduly shapes perceptions about corruption and may tend to undercut its importance based on a historical experience of questionable applicability. Moreover, many point out that politics in developed countries—despite the existence of "modern" values—has not disappeared. This hardly supports the optimistic assessment that development eliminates corruption.[29]

Because of these problems, a structural, state-centered approach to corruption is adopted here. It assumes that corruption is a rational act wherein individuals respond to the immediate structure of rewards and punishments. Although the act by definition is illegitimate when gauged according to the dictates of the state's legitimizing ideology, it may be legitimate when considered in the context of organizational interests. As such, corrupt acts tend to reflect the immediate balance of organizational norms and structures. This means that a corrupt act highlights the relative ability of competing organizations to offer and effect sources of mobility and survival and thus shape the road to personal gain.

In one case, for example, a bureaucrat may follow the superior ability of a business to provide a strategy of mobility and survival by accepting a payment for illegally awarding a government contract, whereas in another case, a bureaucrat's demand for an illegal payment for a legal service from a business corresponds to the ability of the bureaucrat to mobilize the authority of his or her position and dictate the terms to the business. Although the organizational interests of the bureaucracy may not necessarily be promoted (although they may be), the structural balance of the organizational forces roughly determines the limits to which members of an organization can promote exclusively their own personal interests.

Three basic propositions derive from this analysis; they are depicted in Figure 1.1 with the vertical axis representing the strength of state organizations and the horizontal axis the strength of social organizations. First, corruption occurs because of an essential structural imbalance between the ability and capacity of the state and social organizations to influence political behavior. Where a balance exists—as in the center portion of the graph—the cross-pressures from the state and social organizations produce a unique situation in which the state represen-

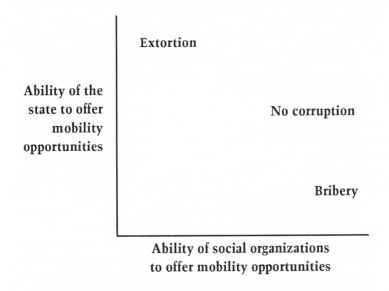

Figure 1.1. State-Society Theory of Corruption

tative's rational pursuit of personal interest parallels the norms of the system. As state and social organizations protect and promote their own interests and attempt to control personal inclinations, the stalemate produced by the cross-pressures results in a nonpoliticized and professional bureaucracy that follows (sometimes religiously) the articulated rules of the political institution and the spirit of the written law; accountable public officials and bureaucrats; and the profusion of modern values antithetical to corruption on a moral and ethical level. For the individual, these unique structural features offer the luxury of pursuing virtuous, altruistic principles.

Second, where the strength of social organizations overshadows that of the state, there is a tendency toward widespread bribery. In this case, it is hypothesized that the ability of social organizations such as businesses, ethnic groups, or even the family, to penetrate the state, thereby illegitimately influencing the conduct of a public official, reflects the superior capacity of these organizations to effect the mobility and survival opportunities of the public official and yet their inability adequately to project their interests as those of the common good.[30]

Finally, in the opposite case, where state organizations are more powerful than social organizations and hence better able to control mobility opportunities (at the upper left-hand portion of the graph), there is a tendency toward widespread extortion. Given the superior ability of state organizations to influence behavior and the concomitant weakness of social organizations to constrain the power of the state, state officials are able fully to exploit their superior position, sometimes exclusively for personal gain. Left in a disadvantageous position, the other member to the corrupt encounter (be it the public at large in the case of autocorruption or a private citizen) is forced to capitulate before the superior power of the state official.

For the sake of theoretical clarity, some additional comments are required. First, state or social organizational strength is defined here as the ability of organizations to offer, effect, and control opportunities for social mobility. This concept refers to more than simply the size of the two or their respective control over resources. Most important, the concept hinges on autonomy. Factors enhancing the power of the state—and hence weakening social organization—for example, can include government centralization, strong internal organizational norms in the bureaucracy, cumbersome legal regulations, a state's monopolistic or monopsonistic position in a particular area of the economy, strict controls over government recruitment, or a monistic ideology. By contrast, a decentralized or fragmented government structure divides the state into competing autonomous state organizations and opens it to the penetration of social organizations. Social organizations, on the other hand, may derive strength from centralization, control of recruitment, ability to offer avenues of wealth, or strong private-oriented ideological appeals.

Although ideology clearly plays a role in the strength of the state, it is possible that the ideology may contain strong and deeply rooted norms opposed to corruption or a strong social orientation that intervenes effectively to thwart the potential for widespread extortion. This intervention may depend on the personal commitment of a leader or on particular tenets of a prevailing ideology. Some point to this factor to explain the apparent absence of upper-level corruption in many communist countries such as Cuba, the Soviet Union, and North Vietnam. Although in these cases the state is clearly dominant and low-level corruption is often widespread, the strength of the anticorruption component of the legitimizing ideology prevents a greater abuse of power. Certain structural factors such as the absence of private wealth in such societies foment this tendency.[31]

The state-centered approach elaborated here overcomes certain weaknesses noted earlier by uniting a host of causal factors from prior theories and differentiating their effects. For example, the idea of a strong state links internal factors of the state (e.g., centralization) to linkages between the state and society (e.g., lack of avenues to wealth in the private sector) to certain aspects of society (e.g., poverty). By differentiating the two broad patterns of corruption, the approach also incorporates previously contradictory hypotheses. It suggests that centralization (adding to a strong state) relates to one type of corruption (extortion), decentralization (weak state) to another (bribery).

Finally, the role of values in this approach should be explicit. As with the critiques of modernization theory mentioned earlier, the existence of values underlying corruption is neither denied nor ignored here; rather, except for the special role of ideology, the notion of causality is. Indeed, corruption may manifest a clash between traditional and modern political orientations, but it does not result from this clash. Instead, values express a proclivity or an antipathy toward corruption where the proper structural conditions exist. Culture and values may be a transmission belt along which corruption is perpetuated, but they are not the root cause. This approach thus tries to look beyond the value orientations to uncover their structural determinants.

The Consequences of Corruption

The second theoretical question centers on the functions or consequences of corruption. This theme, particularly corruption's relationship to political stability and development, stands at the core of much scholarly debate.[32] Given its moral connotations, the notion that corruption is wrong and hence without positive consequence has always been prominent;[33] but a number of analysts, working under the banner of functionalism, identify salient tonic contributions of corruption. They contend, for example, that despite its obvious effects on efficiency and management, corruption functions to integrate a divided elite, facilitate the hidden political influence of a nonsanctioned group, and even promote the needed accumulation of capital.[34]

But though corruption may help buy off important members of the elite, ensuring that they follow the unwritten rules of the inside political game, such practices and rules are, by definition, inconsistent with the guidelines of the legitimizing ideology; for this reason, Gunnar Myrdal suggests that corruption can lead to military coup.[35] This is the crucial paradox concerning the functionality of corruption: if corruption involves behavior inconsistent with the state's legitimizing ideology, then to what degree does corruption erode the legitimacy of the government or its personnel? If corruption provides a vehicle for the illegitimate enrichment of a group of elites, how can this group continue to draw its authority from a state that is legitimized on contrary principles of conduct? If corruption erodes the legitimacy of the state, to what extent and under what conditions does corruption result in protest and mobilizations?

It is important to recall the differentiation between acts that exclusively promote the interests of the state's personnel and those that also promote the interests of the state organizations (both of which derive from the relative strength of state organizations) in treating the issue of consequence. In the latter, illegitimate acts may further the organizational interests of the state's apparatus (its stability) and therefore conform to informal organizational rules.

On one hand, then, corruption contributes to organizational stability by helping foster accommodation, a stable "co-optive" system of spoils, and by discouraging the mobilization of opposition because "its logic and incentives emphasize the divisible over the shared, the tangible over the intangible and the immediate over the long term."[36] Yet on the other hand, corruption produces widespread bureaucratic inefficiency and waste that compromises the legitimacy of these same state organizations. Funds destined for social programs are diverted to and by those the system best serves. By promoting organizational ends contrary to those defined by the legitimizing ideology, corruption negates the impact of government programs.

Pervasive corruption produces a pernicious "culture of corruption" among the public that includes widespread distrust and cynicism toward public officials. Combined with the negation of government programs wrought by corruption, this distrust greatly magnifies the potential loss of legitimacy that sustains the state's organizations. By engendering distrust and thwarting the realization of societal goals, the constant abuse of authority has the potential to undermine authority to such an extent that there may no longer be authority, that is, legitimate power, to abuse.

Clearly, the loss of trust in government can undermine the state's legitimacy and thus holds the potential for instability. But this does not occur if these feelings are not targeted to the organizational components of the state. The normative dimension of corruption can often result in avoiding and redirecting such targeting of frustration. Since corruption is perceived and touted by the authorities as a personal rather than a systemic problem ("a few bad apples"), the government can identify corruption as the cause of its inability to achieve the objectives delineated by the legitimizing ideology, use it as a scapegoat mechanism to detract attention and blame from other, more divisive and destabilizing issues, and focus blame on individual rather than systemic problems. Publicly attacking corruption not only enjoys popular support but implies that with honest politicians, recalcitrant social problems could be resolved.[37] Moreover, government can mobilize popular support to fight corruption so as to rejuvenate faith in the moral integrity of public office and "root the society of evil."[38] By symbolically manipulating the normative meaning of corruption, the government can divert accountability, dodge ideological questions, and target social frustration toward less destabilizing arenas.

Central to the idea linking corruption to stability is the somewhat paradoxical nature of corruption with regard to change. A distinctive feature of corruption is its ability to promote the status quo by altering government programs at the implementation stage and rewarding important government clients (having an impact among the elite), while simultaneously allowing the government to appear responsive to popular demands through the development of popularly supported policy (including demands for an end to corruption), and thus evince the appearance of supporting change. In other words, corruption allows a government the luxury of changing nothing while giving the appearance of promoting change.

For corruption to contribute to stability in this way two conditions are generally required. First, corruption must be maintained within certain limits, thereby ensuring some form of government control.[39] Without this limitation, no government structure could survive and anarchy would result. The use of the normative dimension of corruption as a "scarlet letter" tactic to purge certain public officials who transgress the lines established in the informal system helps maintain these boundaries. The limits, however, are defined by the organizational norms of the state rather than by legitimizing ideology. Second, the abundance and availability of resources condition corruption's contribution to stability. A large pool of resources not only provides the spoils needed to sustain the system, but a growing economic pie determines the degree of public acceptance of corruption. In a regime that delivers high levels of economic growth, for example, corruption by public officials may be considered merely a nuisance. When the economic fruits decline, the same level of corruption will be viewed with greater suspicion.

Applying the Model to Mexico

The following chapters develop and apply this state-centered model of corruption to the case of Mexico. The three-part model of the state organizes the subsequent examination of Mexican politics broadly conceived in Chapter 2, with analysis centering on the nature of the Mexican state and its manifest inconsistencies. Following this general overview of the system, Chapters 3 and 4 address the causes and consequences of corruption in Mexico within the context of the state-society equation and the issues of popular legitimacy and political stability. Bringing cause and consequence together, Chapter 5 addresses the specific patterns of corruption and anticorruption campaigns during the six-year presidential term known as the *sexenio* and explores more fully the nature of the anticorruption campaign. Chapter 6 then explores public attitudes and opinions toward political corruption in Mexico based on a 1986 survey dealing directly with the issue. Finally, Chapter 7 analyzes the crisis-ridden decade of the 1980s, including the effects of recent political and economic change on the underlying causes and consequences of corruption.

2 Politics in Mexico

The Mexican political system has long been considered unique, almost enigmatically so,[1] which has led to general disagreement over the precise nature of the system. According to Martin C. Needler, "appraisals of the political regime of Mexico vary widely, indeed, bewilderingly."[2] Some fancy a basically democratic interpretation, others a decidedly more authoritarian view.[3] Although the latter assessment has dominated since the mid-1970s, case studies nonetheless reveal a softer, more disaggregated form of authoritarianism in Mexico. Business,[4] the bureaucracy,[5] and universities,[6] for instance, enjoy certain degrees of autonomy; the country consistently ranks relatively high on image indexes of Latin American democracy; and citizens have demonstrated a democratic evaluation of the system, have exhibited pride in it, and have boasted a prodemocratic political culture.[7] Indeed, in contrast to most of its Latin American neighbors, in Mexico the scope and degree of individual liberties are comparatively broad and high, and the Mexican military has long maintained its distance from the political arena.

Just as corruption tends to obscure the true nature of things, the Mexican political system supports a wide range of appearances. It is neither fully democratic nor blatantly authoritarian; public policies are neither wholly capitalistic nor decidedly socialistic; interest groups both mobilize and demobilize; and elections "are neither honest nor completely fraudulent."[8] Indeed, Mexico's seeming political moderation on various fronts tends to undermine the use of easy labels.

This chapter discusses the nature of Mexican politics. Using the three-part model of the state presented in Chapter 1, analysis concentrates first on the basic features and characteristics of the ideological, organizational, and personalistic dimensions of the Mexican state as an aid in setting out the various interpretations of Mexican politics in the literature, highlighting the major debates and controversies along the way, and demonstrating the relative power of the Mexican state. Subsequent attention focuses on the discrepancies separating the various levels of the state, moving toward a resolution of the key contradictions by qualifying the scope of their generalizations. The breaches in what could also be considered formal and informal aspects of the system are crucial not only in understanding how the system functions but also in specifying the place of corruption in the system. Finally, the complementary interaction of the three aspects of the system and how they function to create a unique, highly stable, and seemingly paradoxical political phenomenon are examined. This broad overview is crucial in underscoring the linkages between corruption and other aspects of the system.

Three Levels of the Mexican State

The legitimizing ideology of the Mexican state includes strong strains of liberal democracy, an activist state, nationalism, and the principle of no reelection. The Constitution of 1917, the textbooks used in Mexican public schools, the glowing rhetoric and ambitious policies of the political elite, and even the dominant political culture all reflect these principles;[9] the ideals forge the basis and boundaries of Mexican notions of political legitimacy. The legitimizing ideology, referred to as "the symbolic capital of the Mexican Revolution," is highly coherent, consistent, and unchanging, and enjoys widespread consensus. It is a product of both historical circumstance (the 1910–17 revolution) and conscious policy designed to promote an "official interpretation of history."[10]

The first component of the legitimizing ideology, democracy, refers to elections, individual rights, popular sovereignty, and popular consultation. In Mexico, the historical roots of the democratic tradition date from the triumph of the liberals in the middle of the nineteenth century as reflected in the official glorification of the great liberal leader Benito Juárez. According to Lorenzo Meyer, the liberal victory is officially considered the country's major step toward democracy.[11] Not only did the Constitution of 1857 incorporate the paradigmatic language and organizational paraphernalia of democracy based on the French and U.S. experience, but it also served as the model for the current 1917 Constitution.

A second ingredient in the ideal formula involves an activist, nationalist state. This is exemplified clearly by Articles 27 and 123 of the 1917 Constitution. Article 27 grants subsoil rights, provides the legal and moral basis for land reform, and broadly sanctions the state's role in determining the limits and functions of private property. Article 123 maps out the state's protectorate status over labor. Profit-sharing programs for workers, a system of paid vacations and social security benefits, the establishment of collective *ejido* farms for peasants, and the state's extensive control over public resources through both ownership and regulation also embody and reflect these principles. So well entrenched are these policies that many feel it would be virtual political suicide publicly to discuss the return of oil rights to foreigners, the elimination or reversal of the *ejido* program (land reform sector), or the overt negation of workers' social rights.

The third element of the Mexican legitimizing ideology is the principle of no reelection. This principle, which was paramount in both the rise and fall of the dictator Porfirio Díaz, translates in practice into a total constitutional ban on the immediate reelection to any political position in the Mexican government, including not only chief executives but all seats in the federal and state legislatures.[12]

Also subsumed under the state's legitimizing ideology is the normative dimension of corruption. It holds that the public and private spheres of activity are distinct and that public officials should pursue utilitarian goals. But just as those operating in the name of the state often fail to abide by the ideals nominally guiding behavior, the apparatus of the Mexican state often fails to attain the goals supported by its ideology. But despite the relative futility of the goals in determining outcomes, these principles (e.g., democracy) are nonetheless important in sustaining the system's legitimacy and stability. The same is basically true with respect to political corruption. To understand why the system frequently falters in its pursuit of the goals set out by the legitimizing ideology, it is important to focus on the organizational and personalistic aspects of the state.

The Mexican political system's basic institutional components exist at the organizational level. The organizational model can be characterized generally as authoritarian-corporatist, although it is important to distinguish between a dominant set of institutions and processes and a weaker set. The dominant set includes a highly centralized system of authority focusing on the chief executive, corporatist controls over key social organizations, the dominance of the ruling Institutional Revolutionary party (PRI) over political office and elections, a distinct rule-from-the-top authoritarian tendency, and selective repression. The weaker set of institutions reflects the organizational trappings of liberal democracy, including the nominal separation of powers, federalism, social pluralism, and elections. Although reflecting democratic ideals, these institutions are generally subordinate to the dominant authoritarian-corporatist patterns of Mexican organizational life and thus tend to function in a nondemocratic manner.

A major organizational characteristic of the Mexican system is its extreme centralization of political power in the federal executive.[13] Virtually all government and party decisions from the most mundane to the most important come out of the executive in Mexico City. According to Antonio Ugalde, even local and regional PRI organizations are virtually powerless: all decisions require contact with the Federal District.[14]

In the capital, most of this power is concentrated in the office of the presidency.[15] Many, in fact, view the power of the Mexican president to be virtually unlimited, and literary parallels are often drawn between the president, old Aztec emperors, and Spanish kings. Mexican presidents enjoy so much power that for more than a half-century they have hand-picked their own successors following a six-year reign and have generally left office wealthier than when they entered.

In addition to the profound centralization of power around the institutional presidency, a second dominant feature of the organizational design is the corporatist structuring of interest representation.[16] The ruling PRI, often considered the quintessential corporatist organ, counts three sectors: labor, peasant, and popular. Numerous officially sanctioned organizations such as industrial unions are tied to one of these three sectors. By structuring participation from above, such corporate arrangements tend to restrict and channel opportunities for change and for corrupt wealth.[17] As Susan K. Purcell and John F. H. Purcell note, "Corporate structures . . . are less a reflection of Mexican society or even key political alliances, than they are a technique of control developed by the association of ruling groups."[18] One analyst refers to the PRI as a form of "political mobilization in order . . . to demobilize."[19]

The PRI incorporates mainly the lower sectors through such

dependent organizations as the Mexican Confederation of Workers (CTM) and the National Confederation of Peasants (CNC) and segments of the middle class through the National Confederation of Popular Organizations (CNOP). Other groups outside the fold of the official party remain subject to corporatist controls stemming from the government. The three chambers of industrialists and commercial interests, National Confederation of Chambers of Industry (CONCAMIN), National Chamber of Industries of Transformation (CANACINTRA), and National Confederation of Chambers of Commerce (CONCANACO), for example, are functionally specific organizations sanctioned by the state to represent the interests of business in its dealings with the state. Although exercising far greater autonomy than labor or peasant organizations, these organizations nonetheless conform to the dominant corporatist framework of the system by restricting the number of access points to the government.

In a slight variation on the corporatist theme, other nominally autonomous sectors such as the press, opposition political parties, the church, and even intellectuals also depend on the government in one form or another for their well-being. Like more direct forms of corporatism, this dependence often helps mute and temper their opposition to the government. The press, for example, though formally uncensored, nonetheless engages in a sort of autocensorship given that the government controls its supply of newsprint through the state firm PIPSA (although slated for privatization in 1990) and from 25 to 30 percent of its advertising revenues.[20] Even certain opposition parties and a wide range of intellectuals depend on the system for their very survival.[21]

The third feature of the organizational system is the electoral dominance of the PRI. Since its formation in 1929 by President Plutarco Elías Calles (1924–28), the PRI and its predecessors have "officially" won all presidential elections, every seat in the federal Senate save one until 1988 (when the PRI lost four seats to the Cárdenas Front), all governorships until the admitted victory of Ernesto Ruffo in Baja California in 1989, and the vast majority of the seats in the lower federal chamber, state legislatures, and municipalities.

A complex and paradoxical institution, the PRI is both intensely ideological (embodying the goals and ideals of the Mexican Revolution) and highly pragmatic (exhibiting virtually all political tendencies and open to all).[22] Its functions are both broad—it serves as recruiter, broker, integrator, an aggregator of diverse interests, and a mobilizer of popular diffuse support or "symbolic" support for the regime[23]—and extremely circumscribed in the area of policy making. Rather than being a governing party (as in the Soviet Union), the PRI concentrates only on the electoral and recruitment functions, remaining otherwise subservient to the executive and the government bureaucracy.[24] The party, of course, is never mentioned in the Constitution.

The weaker set of institutional structures—although ideally operationalizing the democratic goals—are actually subordinate to these themes of executive control, corporate party discipline, and authoritarianism. Despite official rhetoric and ambitions to the contrary, the separation of powers or federalism is virtually meaningless in any functional sense. Because both branches of Congress are controlled by PRI majorities, Congress has historically served as a virtual rubber stamp to presidential desires.[25] Prior to the presence of opposition parties in Congress following electoral reforms in the 1960s and 1970s, schemes of "proposed" legislation from the executive often escaped with minimal debate and near unanimous approval.[26] Consequently, there are few congressional c˙ ˙cks on the exercise of executive power.

A imilar situation characterizes the relationship of the executive ˙) the judiciary and state and local governments. Not only does tɹ ˙ president appoint the principal personnel of the courts, but he c.˙n easily remove judges for "bad conduct" with only a majority vote in Congress.[27] The president also holds the upper hand with state and local governments, appointing and removing public officials virtually at will.[28] As Meyer asserts, "The entire political life of a governor is controlled by the center, from his nomination by the Party to the selection of his successor."[29] Despite promises to the contrary and seemingly antithetic to his program of "modernization," Salinas had by the end of 1989 removed a host of state governors by decree.[30]

Finally, Mexican elections, although considered the quintessential democratic institution, function differently within the authoritarian-corporatist organizational model. To a large extent, corporatist structures channel political rewards so as to produce PRI electoral victories (similar to the city machine), and authoritarianism translates into the use (at times widespread) of electoral fraud to shape the desired outcome. Neither totally honest nor totally fraudulent, Mexican elections represent in practice something besides a vehicle for the popular expression of political will. Part of the success of the Mexican regime had been to keep the elections free of politics.

By centralizing political mobility within the state and controlling the mobilization of social organizations, the Mexican state tends to hold a preponderance of power in society. As will be shown in Chapter 3, widespread political corruption flows from this essential structure of the system. In other words, the basic authoritarian-corporatist organization of the system encourages behavior inconsistent with the goals of the system's legitimizing ideology. But corruption is a behavioral phenomenon, not an organizational one; its prevalence hence underscores the centrality of personalistic politics in Mexico.

Although most works on Mexican politics underscore centralization, corporatism, or the dominance of the PRI, many have gone beyond the formal organizational trappings of the system to uncover an important, complex, and ubiquitous personalistic system.[31] As the Purcells conclude, there is "little sense of collective solidarity [in Mexico]; rather, individualism or personalistic interactions . . . predominate."[32]

The personalistic system constitutes the third dimension of the state, and it is in this closed and isolated setting that corruption abounds. At this level, corruption, patron-clientelism, personalism, *equipos*, and *camarillas*, political entrepreneurs, middlemen, co-optation, and other modes of personal interactions dominate Mexican politics.[33] The predominance of these particularistic modes both facilitates corruption and structures corrupt political deals.

Personalistic politics in Mexico pervades both interelite and elite-mass relations. By far the clearest and best documented of these involves the role of personalism among the political elite. In an elaborate "pyramid of patronage," [34] political careers revolve around personal loyalties. As Guillermo de la Peña argues, "The rules of the game are . . . a function of personal protection by a patron."[35] Political participants are generally tied vertically to a powerful patron and a host of clients through *equipos* (teams) and *camarillas*. These nuclei of "old-boy networks" exchange loyalty to superiors for patronage and other benefits as they follow their chosen patron from one political post to another in a constant reshuffling of PRI, electoral, and government positions. Considering the electoral dominance of the PRI, the large role of government in society, and the notable lack of a civil service system, the sheer quantity of the system's spoils, including the opportunities for corrupt gains, is magnificent.

The most comprehensive picture of this side of Mexican politics is offered by Peter H. Smith in a detailed and imaginative study that traces political careers through a clientelistic labyrinth and articulates a series of perhaps unarticulated norms or rules for political success.[36] Among them are to select leaders of *camarillas* or political cliques with care, study law at the National University, refer decisions upward, treat subordinates kindly, and avoid controversy.

Beyond the interelite system, this personalistic style of politics also informs government-citizen interactions. As many studies demonstrate, political demands in Mexico are often articulated outside of the formal organizational contexts and through personal contacts and, of course, often via the exchange of personal favors (corruption). Wayne A. Cornelius's study of the migrant poor in Mexico City, for example, found that only 11.5 percent of those interviewed preferred to channel their demands through the PRI: the majority considered it more fruitful to contact bureaucratic officials personally.[37] Similarly, Ugalde discovered that in Ensenada, Baja California, neither unions nor federal bureaucrats employed the party or the CNOP (the popular sector of the PRI) to articulate its demands, opting instead for personal contacts in the government. Contrary to popular belief, his analysis uncovered very little involvement in the official organizations of the party at the local level.[38] Though certainly not all such personalistic politics are corrupt, the pattern brims with the potential for corrupt transactions.

The role of personalism in the government's relations with peasants, business, and potentially powerful social organizations is also widespread. David Ronfeldt, for example, discusses the pervasive personalism of the party in dealing with peasants, particularly the importance of having access to party officials to influence policy among the peasants. Similarly, Dale Story notes a ubiquitous "personalistic style of influence" between government and the business community.[39] Although few have placed particular emphasis on corruption in these studies, it nonetheless greatly informs these personalistic dealings.

Finally, personalism and its attendant corruption pervade the state's relationship to the leaders of large "social" organizations. It has long been recognized that a principal modus operandi of the Mexican political system is for Mexican leaders to go to extensive lengths personally to co-opt the leaders of important organizations such as labor unions, peasant organizations, or even neighborhood associations. This strategy of co-optation involves extracting qualified support for the regime from dissidents in return for a hearing of their concerns and some concessions.[40] In the labor sector, the pejorative term *charro* is widely used to describe the selling out of labor officials to the government. A similar arrangement finds leaders of peasant organizations enjoying personal gains at the expense of any gains to the peasant rank and file.[41] Obviously, political corruption is an important device in the tactical strategy of co-optation.

Given the patron-client networks of the political elite, the use of personal channels to articulate demand, the personal co-optation of organizational leaders, as well as the widespread practice of corruption that frequently characterizes these secretive personal exchanges, there can be little doubt of the fundamental importance of personalism for the Mexican system. Indeed, subsequent analysis will show corruption to be a major factor in facilitating such political tactics and thereby stabilizing the closed elitist system by "buying" political support or acquiescence. But viewed in isolation, such a personalistic system of government appears chaotic, uncontrollable, and totally devoid of morality or guidance. This is because the partial view is misleading; personalistic politics represent just one part of a delicate balance between the ideal, organizational, and personalistic levels of a single political system. It is to the contradictions and interrelationships between the three to which attention now turns.

Contradictions and Interactions

The first task in examining the interactions of this seemingly paradoxical nationalist-democratic, authoritarian-corporate, and clientelistic system is to identify and resolve the major contradictions. Of course, a contradiction exists only when competing interpretations try to explain a common outcome; hence, resolving a contradiction may merely require greater specificity so that the two interpretations apply to two different aspects of the system.

The above model features two salient contradictions. One divides the legitimizing ideology and organizational levels and relates to the democratic/authoritarian thesis referred to earlier. Essentially, it centers around the question of how the system can be democratic in idea yet authoritarian in practice. The second separates the organizational and personalistic levels and centers, to a large extent, on the debate over the power of the Mexican president. It revolves around the question of whether power is centralized, as suggested by the authoritarian-corporate structure, or decentralized, as illustrated by the pervasive personalistic system. Clearly, these two contradictions parallel the incongruence between norm and behavior described earlier with regard to political corruption.

The first contradiction involves the democratic/authoritarian theme. Most students of Mexican politics have encountered this striking gap between the ideal democratic facade and the authoritarian-corporatist reality; most emphatically acknowledge the incredible rift between form and substance when discussing the Mexican case.[42]

Although many analysts discuss the role of ideology and ritual in the system for the elites, the special circumlocutory style of public speaking known as "Cantinflesco," and the importance of using the "revolutionary" language for successful political careers,[43] few have sufficiently resolved the central question: how does the Mexican political elite deal with the democratic/authoritarian paradox? Rephrased, the question ponders how the Mexican elite can constantly and consistently bow to the democratic ideals of the system and the fidelity of ineffective democratic institutions while operating and enjoying the benefits of an authoritarian-corporatist reality.

Apparently the most prominent approach to account for the

gap (since the system cannot be both democratic and authoritarian at the same time)—and often to explain the widespread corruption—is to treat the ruling elite as hypocrites engaged in a massive and well-orchestrated campaign of deception for purely egoistic purposes. This can be referred to simply as the hypocritical or conspirational thesis. Of the many examples of this line of reasoning, Luis Villoro states: "The real meaning of the words remains the concealment, to serve in practice a contrary objective. A revolutionary language is able to be turned into an instrument of conservatism. . . . It [the political language] is used . . . to deceive and thus for power to dominate."[44]

The hypocritical thesis holds sway not only among journalists and politicians but also among scholars. Judging the system based on system outcomes, for example, Roger D. Hansen concludes that "the gap between the governing elite's rhetorical dedication to the social goals of the Mexican Revolution and the resources it has allocated toward their fulfillment can *only* be explained by an interpretation of Mexican politics sharply at odds with those which stress government commitment to 'nation-building,' 'democratization,' and 'social justice'" (emphasis added). Although apparently hard-pressed, Kenneth M. Coleman seems to arrive at a similar conclusion: "It is hard to believe that Mexico's inequality of income distribution is a product of inability to control the private sector and not substantially the result of *conscious* design" (emphasis added).[45]

Explanations besides hypocrisy can be found to account for the gap, however. In discussing Mexico's past, for example, many acknowledge the objective need to go beyond the system's ideals so as to achieve those same goals without indicting the sincerity of the political leaders. Raymond Vernon, for instance, underscores how the Juárez liberals, despite their ideological affinity for decentralization and federalism, were forced to use centralized control to eradicate barriers to a free internal market. Perry Ballard similarly points to such factors as the lack of popular democratic training, capital, infrastructure, and government funds to explain the antidemocratic tendencies of the Juárez government.[46] Neither, however, depicts Juárez as a ruthless dictator who behind the facade sought personal enrichment.

Extending this line of reasoning to the current Mexican elite, one may posit that the elite does not see the authoritarian reality of the system as contradicting its democratic ideals but rather views the authoritarian tendencies of the system as the organizational means needed to achieve the idealized ends. As James Cockcroft notes, "The idealized pictures of the PRI given by informants were . . . normative models of political reality, and these can co-exist, within the same mind, with an accurate descriptive model of sordid reality."[47] In contrast to a more Western, Hegelian view of ideals as an expression of the social environment, then, the democratic ideals of the Mexican Revolution are viewed in a more Kantian manner as "the progressive development of ideas in an endless march toward equality and democracy."[48]

By separating the normative from the real, the elite therefore comes to view stability and orderly change from above as the sine qua non of achieving, albeit in small incremental steps, the democratic and egalitarian goals of the revolution. Though committed in principle to substantial pluralism, the leadership is nonetheless determined to maintain de facto political power, treat autonomous organizations as a political threat, and not succumb publicly to the demands of major organizations.[49] This implies a crisis-management interpretation of Mexican politics in which the ruling elite is committed to long-term transformation as a major government objective but, in its efforts to maintain order and stability, generally unable to effect such changes.[50] As we will see, many political leaders cite corruption as a major factor undermining the impact of sound government policies.

Underlying this crisis-management view is the saliency and overriding concern for political stability in Mexico. Many see Mexico brimming with the potential for extreme political fragmentation that historically has been successfully checked only by centralization.[51] Roderic Ai. Camp, for instance, finds an emphasis on peace and order rather than ideology crucial in informing the broad value consensus among the political elite. Vincent L. Padgett characterizes the postrevolutionary system as a pragmatic venture in accommodating the elite.[52] Such goals may differ from those enlightened by the legitimizing ideology and may even involve tolerating a certain level of corruption for the sake of pragmatism.

Turning to how the public deals with the apparent contradiction, it is important to ask first whether the masses acknowledge the contradiction between what the government says (its guiding ideals) and what it does and how the system has endured despite this realization. To a certain extent, these questions are important in analyzing how the public's interpretation of corruption in the government affects feelings of legitimacy and thus political stability.

There is little doubt that the masses are cognizant of the paradox or the glaring gap between form and substance. Like the elite, the masses "entertain both a descriptive and a normative model of their political system."[53] Popular opinion surveys conducted in Mexico show a seemingly perplexing mix of pride in and support for the system combined with exaggeratedly low respect for the system's operation.[54]

One interpretation of this contradiction is that the public differentiates intentions from reality (as does the elite) and, moreover, the dominant party from the government. Padgett states that the "evidence indicates that loyalty of Mexicans is directed much more toward the nation and revolutionary symbolism than toward the ruling elite."[55] One study found little relationship between popular evaluations of policies (ideals) and services delivered; support for the system was tied to a positive evaluation of the PRI, and negative evaluations of the government were linked to poor government performance. This means that the PRI mobilizes popular support around the popular nationalist-democratic ideals of the system and enjoys an association with those goals, while the government receives the blame for the system's poor performance. In evaluating these findings, the analyst concluded: "The major determinant of loyalty to the political system may well not be the accomplishments of the regime but rather perceptions of intentions." He goes on to suggest that this helps explain why popular support remains "relatively high despite objectively inadequate regime performance in redressing existing inequities of wealth and power."[56]

Another survey, conducted by Mitchell A. Seligson and John A. Booth, confirmed the absence of any strong, direct relationship between diffuse support for the system and evaluation of government performance. Even after correcting for the various problems of prior measures of support for the system and using a superior methodological device, the researchers confirmed a relatively high level of support combined with prodemocratic values. In other words, they discovered a citizenry that simultaneously entertained democratic values and yet supported an authoritarian political system. Noting that the prodemocratic values "harmonize with the current official political ideology," they concluded that the public's "democratic attitudes may ironically both result from and help sustain the very authoritarian and undemocratic system under which they live."[57]

In Chapter 4 I will more clearly set out how corruption has helped the government reaffirm and mobilize support for the system while focusing public cynicism and distrust on the personalistic side of the system, that is, casting the problem as a "few bad apples." In addition, my analysis will concentrate on whether government performance and diffuse support for the system continued to be unrelated during the turbulent changes of the 1980s or whether the rift between form and substance became more problematic than in the past.

The second contradiction of the system underscores even more poignantly the place of corruption and pits a centralized authoritarian-corporatist organizational system with a strong president against a decentralized, flexible, and accommodative personalistic system with a weak president. Clearly, references to corruption, the effective influence of certain individuals at the implementation stage of public policy, the accommodations of major clients in the bureaucracy, and the important role of the bureaucracy in policy making (all conducive to political corruption) depict a system contrary to the "formal" one described as centralized on an omnipotent president.[58]

Meyer provides a good illustration of this paradox. He describes centralized presidential power as almost unlimited ("No matter how irrational a project may be in the eyes of specialists, if the president approves it, it must be carried out"). Yet in alluding to corruption, he refers to a bureaucracy unable to carry out policy effectively. But how powerful is a president who cannot effectively implement policy? Richard S. Fagen and William S. Tuohy also point to the paradox: "Any rationalization or coordination of Mexican public policy that might result from centralization is lost through the corruption, inefficiency, and personalistic careerism that are the other side of the centralization coin."[59] Again the question arises of whether the system is centralized or decentralized.

Since the system cannot be both, nor can the president possess virtually unlimited power and yet be circumscribed by an intransigent or corrupt bureaucracy, the contradiction begs for greater specificity. Rather than blatantly and categorically viewing the system as centralized or decentralized, one must recognize the areas in which centralized presidential power pertains and those in which decentralized power is the norm. Generally, centralized presidential power occurs primarily in areas of recruitment and policy initiative, whereas decentralized bureaucratic and particularistic influences dominate the actual implementation of public policy. The president's centralized control involves the more public side of the political equation (broad policy programs, political appointments, and rhetorical campaigns), whereas the decentralized decision-making process encompasses the more private and closed personalistic side of the system. Though the president may direct anticorruption campaigns, for example, gain the prosecution of certain high-level officials, or even set out the boundaries for corrupt activities, he is severely constrained in his ability truly to curb the political corruption that pervades the accommodative elitist system. Generally, this balance between the two enhances the stability of the governmental system.

Having resolved these contradictions, we may now explore the complementary nature of the three aspects of the system. Historically, the three have functioned in concert, providing a stable political environment. The legitimizing ideology carries popular legitimacy, the organizational system contains popular mobilizations and structures clientelistic relationships, and the personalistic system obviates "the formal and public exercise of political controls" by channeling particularistic demands toward a highly flexible system of implementation.[60] The role of the PRI and the Mexican governing style demonstrate the fundamental nature of the system.

A good illustration of the interaction of the three levels of the Mexican state revolves around the multiple functions of the PRI. First, the PRI incorporates the legacy of the Mexican Revolution, monopolizes and promotes the revolutionary myth, and thus serves as a vehicle for the legitimizing ideology. In this sense, the PRI is much more than a political party; it contains strong nationalist undertones. For many Mexicans (and *priístas*), the PRI is the embodiment of the nation: its colors are the colors of the flag. Second, the PRI mobilizes the people into populist organizations, the existence of which lends credence to their revolutionary goals but simultaneously allows the upper elite to control the articulation of political demands from below. The system's corporate controls over the press and intellectuals even further enhance the regime's ability to perpetuate the PRI's monopoly on patriotic ideals.[61] Third, monopolistic control over the system's ideals combined with strong patronage rolls translates into electoral victories for the party (with electoral fraud playing a backup role) and hence control of government personnel. By controlling recruitment and government personnel, the PRI thus dominates the personalistic side of the system. It administers a secure and permanent spoils system for those willing to abide by the political rules of the game.[62] The spoils include not only political appointment but the attendant opportunities for corrupt wealth that flow from an activist state.

A second illustration of the interactions relates to the Mexican style of governance: the government's ability to fend off attacks from opponents by crippling the capacity of horizontally based organizations and transforming divisive political issues into administrative haggles. The PRI's monopoly over the system's ideals (patriotism, democratic legitimacy, and so on) provides the government with significant political capital to offset threats to its organizational authoritarian/corporatist control. This is accomplished by manipulating revolutionary and nationalist symbols so as to mobilize popular support and thus undercut the appeals of any opposition movement or horizontal organization that may desire greater autonomy. The government thus alters coalitions and alliances to offset the attacks of other sectors.[63] The government can cast the rightist opposition as antinationalistic and antirevolutionary by rhetorically linking it to such antirevolutionary symbols as the church or the United States. The government has often directed public campaigns depicting the Mexican business community as engaging in anti-Mexican activities.

The effective control of the PRI and the government over organizational channels combined with the relative effectiveness of the personalistic system to accommodate particularistic demands effectively inhibits members from using the group as a vehicle to serve collective interests.[64] As one analyst notes, "Approaching public officials to seek help in satisfying particularistic personal or local needs is both permitted and encouraged; but demanding major changes in public policy or government priorities is viewed as threatening and illegitimate activity."[65]

Since diffuse support has in the past been unrelated to government performance, the resulting gaps between policy intention and actual bureaucratic output would not seem to compromise the system's overall legitimacy. Consequently, it is possible that administrative policy (and corruption) can accommodate major client groups and serve the goals of stability and the maintenance of the status quo rather than the objectives of development or social justice.[66]

Vernon offers a good example of this "double-faced" style of governance. Noting government's control of pharmacy prices, Vernon recounts a case in which the pharmaceutical company made a strong and convincing argument to the government for a price increase. Finding it politically unwise to be publicly associated with such an unpopular move, the government quietly advised the company that if it were to violate the law by raising prices, the infraction would be ignored. In this way, the government attended to its public image of controlling prices and maintained the support of the industry.[67]

A final aspect of the Mexican governing style is the process of reducing political questions to administrative ones, thereby avoiding conflict. This practice stems from the duality in which the president has virtually unlimited control over policy direction but leaves the specifics of implementation to the dynamics of the personalistic system, which can accommodate particularistic demands. Susan Purcell found that although the push for a Mexican profit-sharing program originated with labor, President Adolfo López Mateos (1958–64) adopted the policy as his own to protect the tradition of centralized control. Once having made the fundamentally political decision that there would be a profit-sharing program, however, he turned the details of the program over to an advisory committee representing all affected parties (business, labor, and government). In this way, the parties that were excluded at the policy-making stage were incorporated into the less public implementation stage.[68]

Corruption is a crucial mechanism in Mexico's unique governing style. By allocating spoils, corruption helps undermine the potential of organizations to threaten the system and thus helps alleviate class-based demands. Although widespread corruption may result in low levels of trust in the performance of government, the goals of the system or the policies of the government may not be questioned. Indeed, blaming human avarice for the system's failures provides an easy escape for the government, thereby taming a potentially politically explosive issue.

3

The Causes of Corruption in Mexico
The State-Society Balance

This chapter argues that corruption in Mexico stems from a structural imbalance of state and social forces that effectively grants the Mexican state and its representatives a virtual monopoly over opportunities for wealth and mobility. This structural asymmetry foments a particular pattern of corrupt behavior characterized by widespread extortion. The first part of the chapter identifies the principal structural traits of state and society promoting corruption; the latter section examines hundreds of cases featured in the Mexico City press from 1970 to 1984.

The State-Society Equation

In Mexico, the state dominates the structuring of opportunities for mobility, which in turn fosters the conditions favorable to widespread political corruption. Three parts of the equation can be discerned: attributes internal to the state, linkages between the state and society, and general factors of society.

A large ingredient of the state's strength vis-à-vis society derives from internal attributes ranging from the basic structure of the government and the role of the PRI to the state's laws covering its employees and bureaucratic procedures. Of fundamental importance, the Mexican state projects a single, centralized avenue of social mobility: a monolith. Rapid turnover in public office, the prohibition against reelection, and a dominant executive branch all serve to solidify this monopolistic pattern. This structure, in turn, enhances the possibilities for widespread political corruption by sustaining an upward-flowing pattern of political loyalty.

Control over recruitment in the vast Mexican public sector resides with the top political elite in the PRI and the government. Few alternative poles attracting talent and inspiring loyalty in the public sector compete with the centralized control of the party and the bureaucracy. Only one route to social advancement within the state is available. As a result, most employees of the government are dependent on their good standing in the party or among upper level officials for any opportunities for mobility.

The prominent juridical classification "employees of confidence" underscores the fact that position and political future rest squarely on sustaining that confidence. One study of the Ministry of Water and Public Works, for example, revealed that 75 percent of the employees of the agency were classified as confidence employees and that "who one knows" was the key to their employment.[1]

A high turnover rate, a constant shuffling of positions within the government, and the dominance of the executive branch over the other branches of government further enhance this monopolistic control of mobility opportunities in one party, thereby consolidating the power of the state. Most Mexican officials rarely occupy the same post for more than a single administrative term. Hansen estimated that eighteen thousand elective and twenty-five thousand appointive positions in the Mexican government changed hands every six years; another report placed the estimate at forty-five thousand top posts.

According to Smith, about a third of all public positions in the government are affected by turnover and reshuffling from one *sexenio* to another. In elective positions, of course, incumbency is illegal. But even in the bureaucracy, such constant movement is normal. Guillermo Kelley states: "In the US public servants tend to make a career in a particular bureau or agency, whereas in Mexico they are horizontally mobile, serving in a wide range of positions throughout the bureaucracy."[2] This turnover is even common at the local level, resulting in highly unstable bureaucratic directorships.[3] These high turnover rates strongly impinge on feelings of job security (or insecurity) and reinforce the importance of maintaining the confidence of one's superiors.

The imbalances that characterize relations between the federal, state, and local governments and the executive, legislative, and judicial branches further compound the centralized, monopolistic route of state-centered mobility. Rather than exercising autonomous power—and thus checking the power of the executive or offering alternative poles of social advancement within the state—these institutions are incorporated into the patron-client labyrinth and depend on the executive either for their institutional or individual political survival. Because of the prohibition on reelection, members of Congress, for instance, must look to the centralized apparatus of the party and the patron-client networks of the bureaucracy for their next political appointment. A similar structural arrangement characterizes the relationship between the judiciary and the executive and between state and local governments and the federal government.

The effect of such a monopolistic avenue of political fortune on bureaucrats or members of Congress, is to reinforce loyalty upward toward a centralized source and away from clients, constituents, particular bureaucratic ethos, or alternative poles of loyalty.[4] This process occurs through two mechanisms. First, because future employment is not assured, the bureaucrat or politician must constantly nurture his political relationships to enhance future employment prospects. Second, the bureaucrat cannot develop contacts, expertise, or sympathy with and for the clients of a particular bureau or agency or with constituents because of the limited time of the appointment and the futility of doing so. He or she has little sense of bureaucratic professionalism, little loyalty to the agency, and no unique political ideology. "The Mexican administrator does not consider himself tied to administrative performance nor bound by a code of administrative conduct enforced legally and socially by his peers. His loyalty is to his superior."[5]

Together, these factors underpin strong internal norms (both written and unwritten) that facilitate widespread corruption. The high turnover rates and lack of job security (combined with inadequate retirement plans) create strong pressures for public officials to devise imaginative personal pension schemes to "prepare for their own exits" from government.[6] The existence of upwardly focused loyalty patterns encourages officials to engage in or acquiesce to corrupt networks within a particular agency. Because their political future rests with higher-ups, few jeopardize any confidence they may have gained by questioning the procedures or exposing the corrupt operating rules of their superiors. Indeed, the only way to survive politically is to abide by the rules of the system and enjoy the benefits of political office. Sharing in corrupt gains often forms a crucial part of the superior's management style because it helps instill a deeper sense of loyalty and dependency among underlings.

Strong internal norms thus essentially force officials to participate in corrupt networks to maintain employment. The head of Consciencia Ciudana, for example, noted that "even kids that enter [a police force] with the best of intentions have to conform to the norm [participate in corruption] or get out." The norm, as described in detail by one police sergeant, usually means the obligatory payment of a portion of a policeman's daily bribes to his superior; or as another officer put it, "all the bosses receive a share from us."[7] Such exploitation of police employees was a fundamental device in the management style of Mexico City police chief Durazo: employment was contingent on payments "up the ladder."

Besides facilitating pyramidal networks of corruption, such factors also forge strong norms against reporting corruption or cooperating in official investigations. The individuals involved must rationally calculate where the better opportunity lies, and in many cases, it resides with supporting one's superior who is suffering attack rather than with those orchestrating the assault. The secretary general of the PRI even admits that the party represses members who do not follow the rules of the game, thus making it hard to denounce others engaged in wrongdoing.[8] Examples of such suppression include the protection offered by the local legislature in Chilapa, Guerrero, to the interests and businesses of its chief executive; the local police chief who shielded his men from investigation; and the successful PRI-led opposition to expanding the investigation of the stock market scandal in 1989 to include higher-ups and the banks.[9] It can even be seen in the handling of denouncements against former presidents López Portillo and De la Madrid.

In addition to fostering unwritten, unarticulated norms promoting corruption, the preponderant strength of the state also translates into weak and ineffective legislation covering corruption or basic bureaucratic procedures. In many cases, the written norms reflect unwritten rules. Thus faulty legal devices add to the potential for corruption by failing to create a structure of deterrence. According to one legal expert, "the Law of Responsibilities—the law pertaining to public officials—is 'an authentic disaster' . . . Mexico lacks an adequate legal structure to combat corruption."[10]

The inadequacies of the law dealing with corruption are twofold. First, the law inhibits the reporting of corruption by outside parties by requiring exorbitant amounts of proof and holding the accuser liable for unsubstantiated accusations. The Comité Coordinador de la Ciudanía, for example, claimed that the Puebla state congress would not permit it to denounce corruption in the state government based on legal technicalities, adding that various members of the group had received threats.[11] Sometimes contributing to the fight against corruption is costly. In July 1984, for instance, a professor of the National University who falsely accused the head of the federal department of education of extortion was arrested for false declarations.[12] The much-touted campaign of reforms under De la Madrid to fight corruption was seen by many as even further hampering the reporting of corrupt acts. The president of the Union de Universidades at the Third Ibero-American Congress of International Law, for example, complained that the new Law of Responsibilities (revised in 1983) "is contradictory since it makes it difficult for citizens to denounce corruption if they cannot prove the charges."[13]

The second legal deficiency relates to the lack of a juridical basis for the punishment of officials charged with malfeasance. Before the 1983 reforms, castigation simply meant returning a portion of the ill-gotten gains to the state. For example, charges of fraud against eighteen officials of the state cinema industry were dropped in 1979 following the return of 120 million pesos. A similar incident brought the release of twenty-six officials convicted of fraud ten days after their arrest when the president of the business returned 2.4 million pesos to the Justice Department.[14] Such mild punishment led the opposition to criticize the law as "rob now and pay later."[15]

In addition to light punishment, the law provides public officials with convenient cushions against prosecution. Officials holding public office enjoy immunity from prosecution, which must be removed before further legal action is taken. Moreover, a "period of responsibility" (or statute of limitations) is stipulated in the law that restricts prosecution for wrongdoing while in office to one year following the official's removal from that post. An effort to increase the limit to four years was defeated in Congress in 1978.[16]

Finally, an important corollary to the punishment factor is that even those punished are often granted opportunities to return to public life. Although the attorney general claims that he provides a list of officials prosecuted to prevent this from happening, the late journalist Manuel Buendía noted at one point that of two thousand public officials prosecuted, half had already returned to public life.[17] One notable case involves the political resurrection of the deposed governor of Sonora, who was removed amid charges of "unexplained wealth"; in the late 1980s he was occupying an important position in the government of the state of Hidalgo.[18] According to Buendía, being branded in this way often evokes respect within the closed elitist circle.[19]

As with the law dealing specifically with corruption, general bureaucratic regulations also seem inadequate to discourage corruption. One report by the Chamber of Deputies, for example, revealed that the Mexico City government from 1976 to 1982 never solicited competitive bids in its public works.[20] Another estimate suggests that about 85 percent of PEMEX contracts were made without competitive bidding as required by law in the late 1970s.[21] Ugalde found that even at the state level, huge sums were spent but very few records were kept and large amounts went for "personal expenses."[22]

Despite the apparent importance of various legal requirements, it remains questionable whether better laws would change anything. An argument can be made that it is not that the laws are bad but that they are ignored. In 1977, legislators of the PRI openly complained that the Law of Responsibilities (despite its shortcomings) had never been enforced.[23] Just as a written constitution does not make a functioning democracy, the proper legal framework could hardly prevent corruption. Corruption is illegal; therefore, the impotency of laws against it is almost tautological. From a different perspective, however, it can be argued that inadequate laws or weak enforcement reflect the lack of alternative, competing avenues of mobility in the state and the relative inability of social organizations to check the power of state officials. In this sense, the law mirrors the structural realities that create the conditions for corruption.

In addition to factors internal to the state, the state-society equation encompasses linkages between the state and society. The internal factors help consolidate the strength of the Mexican state, and the bonds linking it to society further intensify its dominant position. Although traditional indicators of the size of the state in controlling resources vis-à-vis society provide a somewhat mixed picture, a host of other factors such as the strength of the state's legitimizing ideology and its ability to impinge on opportunities for wealth and mobility and corporatism suggest a strong state apparatus. All these together add to the potential for corruption by inhibiting societal checks on state power and by forcing weaker social organizations into exploitable positions vis-à-vis state representatives. A review of business, union, and press corruption helps illustrate this problem.

Although size is hardly synonymous with strength (or autonomy), indicators of the size of the Mexican state reveal a relatively unimpressive apparatus, at least until the 1970s. Until then the state ranked low in cross-national comparisons. Central government expenditures in Mexico totaled 12.2 percent of gross domestic product under President Gustavo Díaz Ordaz (1964–70), 15.9 percent under Echeverría (1970–76), and 26.9 percent under López Portillo (1976–82); expenditures for decentralized state firms accounted for an additional 11.7, 15.4, and 22.6 percent under the three administrations.[24]

Other indicators of size of government, however, provide a somewhat clearer picture. During the mid-1980s, for example, the government employed 4.35 million people or 18 percent of the work force, compared to roughly 16 percent in the United

States.[25] Figures from the mid-1970s also seem to point to a large if not proliferated state. Merilee Grindle notes that the Mexican bureaucracy at that time contained 18 regular ministries and departments, 123 decentralized agencies, 292 public enterprises, 187 official commissions, and 160 development trusts, compared to 17 executive offices, boards, and councils, 11 departments, 59 agencies, 6 quasi-official agencies, and 64 other commissions in the United States.[26] More recent figures show that by 1982, the government controlled a total of 1,214 firms.[27]

Though clearly important, these figures are incomplete if not misleading because they do not take into account the centralization of state power, the autonomy of the state, its ideological mandate, or its regulatory and recruitment controls over other state entities and society. A review of these factors supports the view of a powerful, penetrating state.

For a variety of cultural, historical, economic, and political reasons, Mexico's legitimizing ideology supports a strong interventionist state. The Mexican state shoulders responsibility for administering, directing, and guiding the developmental process, guaranteeing social justice, aiding the private sector in its disadvantageous relationships with foreign capital, and forging social harmony and peace among all sectors of society. Such an ideological posture has resulted in the state's ownership of some of the nation's largest enterprises (PEMEX, CFE [electricity], and Teléfonos de México), its control over large portions of the nation's savings to finance development, extensive laws and bureaucratic regulations touching virtually all areas of social life—especially organizational life—and a correspondingly weak tradition for the notions of pluralism.[28]

Although the Mexican Revolution accentuated these trends, Mexico has historically enjoyed a strong, domineering state. The Spanish colonial system was paternalistic and bureaucratic, imposing itself on all areas of society. Before the end of the Hapsburg era, "Mexico was governed by an enormous bureaucracy residing many kilometers away," resulting in "an administrative system which was as complex as it was unrealistic."[29]

The activist, organic state is indeed common to all Latin America. But in the case of Mexico, the revolution greatly compounded the power of the state by imbuing the PRI with a substantial dosage of legitimacy and by severely weakening the influence of foreign interests, the church, and landowners. Throughout the postrevolutionary epoch, the power of these groups has remained limited or has grown only under the tutelage of the state.

The formidable position of the state invariably facilitates corruption by strengthening its power in its dealings with major social organizations and by limiting the autonomy of such organizations to offer opportunities for mobility or to check the power of state representatives. Consequently, large portions of the government are left virtually uncontrolled and thus vulnerable to the avaricious proclivities of their employees.

Perhaps the best illustration of an uncontrolled government sector awash in opportunities for mobility is the state-owned petroleum enterprise, PEMEX. Because of the rapid development of the industry in the late 1970s, the large profits flowing from high world prices for oil from 1978 to 1981, and the management problems associated with directing Mexico's largest enterprise, PEMEX exhibited enormous potential for corruption—a potential to which it aspired. Although historically sporting scandal, the flood of cases of corruption in PEMEX in the early 1980s earned it the reputation of being extremely corrupt. As one analyst remarks: "PEMEX is a state enterprise that does practically whatever it wants, passing above the law, regulations and official norms of control and is going through a period of . . . corruption and economic waste and chaos in its internal finances."[30]

Corruption in business, unions, and the press provides further illustrations. The business environment is marked by strong government intervention ranging from the regulations, subsidies, licensing, permits, and exchange-rate brokers to the supplying and purchasing of products. The plethora of administrative devices—what one businessman referred to as *reglamentismo*[31]—augments the contacts between government and business and gives the bureaucrat a broad base of power in dealing with business. Through these devices the state structures the business environment and displaces other rules of entrepreneurship. Since the government is in a position to make or break any private firm,[32] it is often "more important to have good political connections than entrepreneurial skills," a situation referred to by Ben Ross Schneider as "political capitalism."[33] One observer alludes to "a relatively small number of large private sector interests dependent on a favorable relationship with an interventionist government that maintains a huge regulatory apparatus and equally large proprietary holdings."[34]

Because the state holds such a powerful advantage, the payment of bribes by businesses to acquire operating licenses, permits, and other government services becomes routine. Ugalde, for example, found that the bureaucratic chief in the construction industry customarily received a 10 percent "surcharge."[35] One businessman stated that bribes are a routine practice to obtain government permits or to pay judges who refuse to accept papers; another added that bribes were required to speed up the process of paying taxes, to obtain import and export licenses, and even to "arrange" an overcharged bill from the electric company.[36]

The ideological supremacy of the state over business should also be emphasized because it provides a certain degree of acceptance of corruption. Taking from those in an ideologically weak position is generally easy to justify. According to Frank Tannenbaum, "Graft had a kind of traditional sanction when most of the economy was in foreign hands, when government officials shared through special favors some of the profits of private concerns."[37] Although business today is essentially in national hands, the government nonetheless frequently portrays the private sector and its supporters as antinationalistic. Similar to the government's role in shaping the economy, its corporatist links to interest associations serve to enhance its control over opportunities for mobility and thus facilitate corruption among co-opted organizations. Business associations, labor unions, and peasant associations are particularly affected by laws that structure interest representation in Mexico. One effect of such corporative arrangements is to weaken the autonomy of these groups, first, by placing effective decision making and recruitment authority outside of the organization and with the government, and, second, by reducing the opportunities for competing organizations within the same functional area to vie for support of the rank and file. Since government leaders have a powerful say in job security, mobility opportunities, and political futures, corporatist organizations tend to maintain a leadership more attuned to the needs of the government than to those of the rank and file.

This pattern is particularly evident in the Mexican labor movement, where corruption is widespread. In exchange for labor stability, labor leaders enjoy the fruits of subcontracts (often referred to as "sweetheart" contracts), large pension funds, and the control of lucrative public sector jobs and other patronage positions in the government. According to the Movimiento Nacional Petrolero, union leaders in the powerful petroleum workers union (STPRM) use union dues to support their private businesses.[38] The leadership of the STPRM has been involved in a variety of scandals stemming from the sale of jobs, the awarding of contracts to friends and family members, the illegal sale of petroleum on the international black market, and extortion of union funds.[39]

Similar practices among other official unions are common. One report indicated that more than two hundred union leaders of the Mexican Confederation of Workers (CTM) were under investigation for corruption in 1985 alone.[40] As in the government, union corruption reflects the lack of management controls. One union leader charged with corruption, for example, had occupied his post for twelve years without producing a single accounting of union funds, and a union in Veracruz escaped the auditing pen for fourteen years.[41]

The government-press relationship also typifies the state-society asymmetry. This relationship is unique, with the state exercising subtle forms of control and the press exhibiting self-censorship. Corruption forms an important part of the relationship. "Much of what makes government-media cooperation so mutually advantageous involves corruption."[42] According to one observer, the press-government relation is a "vicious circle of corruption": "the *embute* [envelope with money] is a national institution."[43]

As with the business-government relationship, members of the press find it rational to follow the corruption-paved avenue to mobility offered by members of the state rather than attack the system. As Evelyn P. Stevens argues, "It would be an exceptionally courageous publisher—or a very foolish one—who would bite the hand which feeds him."[44]

But besides setting the conditions for mobility possibilities and hence presenting the potential for corruption, the power of the state vis-à-vis society also inhibits the ability of business, unions, and the press to check the power of state officials. One business official bluntly suggested that if one tries to organize and fight, government purchasing contracts will not be renewed.[45] Likewise, the prevalence of state-affiliated unions constrains the formation of independent unions. Although independent labor unions are not illegal, they rarely enjoy the benefits of subcontracting or control over employment in the industry. Without such enticements, it is difficult to praise the prospects of independent syndicates. The press's lack of autonomy also prevents it from protecting its members who attempt to expose corruption or push government toward an incorrupt road. If a member of the press does "bite" the hand, the consequences may be detrimental. The politically inspired removal of the entire editorial board of *Excélsior* in the late 1970s, the firing of the editor of *El Heraldo* in Puebla in 1983,[46] and the killings of more than thirty reporters in the late 1980s all stand as stark reminders of the close control over the press in Mexico.

The third component of the state-society equation involves certain structural features of Mexican society that detract from the ability of social organizations to offer competing routes of social mobility and thereby check the power of the state or the perquisites of its employees. In most respects these factors represent the opposite side of the corporatist and bureaucratic coin and have already been discussed. One analyst sums up this situation: "[The postrevolutionary state] put a brake on the creation of a truly autonomous and vigorous business sector. The union movement was born as an extension of governmental political power in such a way that it lacked authentic autonomy and reproduced the same anti-democratic and corrupt forms of the system. Other sectors such as press, legislative, and judiciary lacked the bases to preserve their autonomy and thus were incorporated into the corrupt system."[47]

Two additional characteristics of society that weaken the capacity of social organizations and enhance the prospects for corruption include the inability of social organizations to provide effective avenues to wealth and the general underdevelopment of organizations in an environment of poverty and inequality. The inability of social organizations to offer an alternative avenue to wealth and mobility has long been associated with corruption.[48] Throughout Mexico's turbulent history, opportunities were either controlled by the Spanish elite, which excluded mestizos or those of mixed origin, or foreign businesses. Historically, corruption was a response "to the lack of opportunities for mobility within the country's economic and social systems."[49] Although other means of wealth are available today, the opulence of the state in a sea of poverty continues to make it an attractive means of acquiring wealth. "The idea of politics is corruption," one observer suggested; "people get into politics to make money."[50]

The weakness of social organizations vis-à-vis the state stems in part from their limited number. The lack of voluntary organizations, which is common in less developed countries, tends to instill a personalistic image of social relations. One observer suggests that corruption is even more readily accepted under such conditions.[51] Whether this is so or not, it is clear that the absence of organizations makes it extremely difficult to pursue collective goals. Although business is strongly opposed to certain corrupt practices, it has generally been unable to articulate its demands properly because of its organizational lack of development.[52]

There are many reasons for the weakness of social organizations in Mexico. Of obvious importance is the lack of social differentiation, time, trust, consciousness, and other characteristics associated with underdevelopment. But one analyst suggests that an "antiorganizational" ethos pervades Mexican society.[53] To an extent, this attitude reflects a conscious policy style on the part of the government designed to discourage organizational formation and block autonomous social organizations, particularly among the lower sectors. An intense fear in the government of "autonomous mobilizations from below" reflects the government's steadfast belief in the need to guide and direct change from above so as to avoid a recurrence of the social convulsions and explosions of the revolutionary period.

Patterns of Corruption in Mexico

Empirical patterns of corruption in Mexico can provide some tests of certain hypotheses derived from the state-society theory. Although not nearly as neat and conclusive as often desired in empirical research, the following data do provide some means of gauging the merits of the theory and moving beyond the anecdotal toward the empirical.

By its very nature, political corruption cannot be measured reliably. One possible proxy indicator of corruption is news information, although even then it is difficult to differentiate between the level of corruption and the quality of reporting. As with criminal statistics, it is difficult to know whether an increase in reports of corruption reflects a higher incidence of corruption or merely an increase in or better reporting. News reports may not be the most reliable means available, but they can be complemented by other methods such as observation, interviews, and public opinion polls.

The data presented here are taken from over nine hundred reports on corruption in the Mexico City press from 1970, 1971, 1972, 1974, and 1976 to 1984. For the years 1970, 1971, 1972, and 1974, a random sample of fifty-two issues of *El Nacional* and *Excélsior* per year was examined and coded. For the years 1976 to 1984, articles were located using *Información Sistemática*, a complete index of virtually all the major newspapers of Mexico City. The news reports were coded for type of article (a case of corruption, a general denouncement of corruption, or promotion of reform measures), type of corruption, organizational affiliation of the parties involved, the denouncing party, the tone of the article (positive or negative), and, finally, the press's characterization of the problem (personalistic, systemic, or attributable to the citizenry). It is expected that the data represent a rough sampling of corrupt acts in the country. The Appendix explicates more fully the methods used for collecting and coding the data.

Table 3.1 categorizes the cases of corruption: "extortion and fraud" denote corrupt acts initiated and executed by government officials against either members of society or government itself; "bribery, private, or collusion" indicates social organizations or private citizens penetrating government through

Table 3.1. Corruption by Category as Reported in the
Mexico City Press, 1970–1984

Category	Number (n = 567)	Percent
Extortion and fraud	314	59.5
Bribery, fraud, and collusion	82	15.6
Land fraud	57	10.8
Contraband, black market, and forgery	29	5.5
Employment-related	18	3.4
Other types	27	5.1

bribes or defrauding either private or public enterprises; "land fraud" entails the illegal sale or use of lands, usually by government officials charged with administering the land reform program; "contraband, black market, and forgery" could include members of either the public or private sector; and "employment-related" acts include the practice of ghost workers (referred to in Mexico as *aviadores*) and the sale of jobs *(plazas)*. The "other" category represents everything not otherwise classified. Cases in which the nature of the act was unclear are not included here.

Table 3.2 classifies the data by bureaucratic or functional location, indicating the defrauded agency or the home agency of the officials involved. Most of the terms are straightforward. Generally, problems of cross-classification (such as how to code cases involving institutions such as BANRURAL, the Mexican agricultural development bank, or cases with multiple actors from different agencies) were handled in an ad hoc fashion. BANRURAL, is a specialized bank, for example, so it was classified under agriculture, though all other banks are un-

Table 3.2. Bureaucratic Locus of Incidences of
             Corruption

Area	Number (n = 567)	Percent
Agriculture	83	14.6
Banking	48	8.5
Communications, transportations, customs	39	6.9
Congress	9	1.6
Education	32	5.6
Commerce, industry, parastate firms	44	7.8
Judicial	10	1.8
Military	4	0.7
PEMEX	34	6.0
Police	51	9.0
Private business	38	6.7
Social welfare	16	2.8
State and local	81	14.3
Unions	38	6.7
Other	40	7.0

der banking. Cases involving multiple actors were coded according to what was judged to be the more important actor to the case.

Finally, Table 3.3 identifies the parties denouncing both specific cases of wrongdoing and those more generally con-

Table 3.3. Parties Denouncing Corruption

Area	Specific Case (n = 310) Number	Percent	General Denunciation (n = 131) Number	Percent
President	0		1	0.8
Justice Department comptroller, police	128	41.3	13	9.9
Same bureaucracy	49	15.8	14	10.7
Other Federal Agency	16	5.2	9	6.9
State and local	8	2.6	5	3.8
PRI/Congress	10	3.2	6	4.6
Opposition parties	7	2.3	19	14.5
Business and professional organizations	7	2.3	7	5.3
Unions	22	7.1	10	7.6
Peasant organizations	24	7.7	6	4.6
Other organizations	27	8.7	19	14.5
Press and other	12	3.9	22	16.8

demning corruption. Three general comments are in order. First, there are fewer cases than in Tables 3.1 and 3.2 because many articles discussed specific cases without mentioning the denouncing party. It is possible that such cases were exposed by the press itself although they were not coded or treated as such unless that conclusion was explicitly supported. Second, certain categories warrant additional explanation. "Same bureaucracy" refers to denouncement originating within the agency or area of the government in which the case occurred (such as the police exposing police corruption); "other federal agency" excludes those specifically listed in the table (the Justice Department, Comptroller, Congress, and so on), including "same bureaucracy"; "other organizations" refers to nongovernment organizations such as citizen groups or ad-hoc, single-purpose interest associations. Finally, PRI and Congress were combined into one category because many articles made generic references to Congress without partisan distinction. Since the Mexican Congress is overwhelmingly controlled by the PRI, any such generic reference was coded under this category. Conversely, any article referring to a member of Congress from an opposition party was coded under "opposition parties" rather than Congress.

The data offer a means to test certain hypotheses. First, the theory suggests that because of the overwhelming power of the Mexican state, the most basic form of corruption in Mexico would be extortion rather than bribery. The data in Table 3.1 indicate that this is the case: extortion and fraud accounted for 59.5 percent of all cases. Although not differentiated, most of these cases involved fraud in which the government official stole from or conspired against his own agency (a form of autocorruption). The level of extortion and fraud is even higher than shown if land fraud is included. By contrast, bribery was much less prevalent, constituting only 15.6 percent of cases. Fiscal fraud seemed to be the most prominent type within this general category.

Besides type of corruption, the theory also suggests that corruption occurs more frequently in bureaucratic areas where the state-society imbalance is the greatest. Although the imbalance is not quantified, the data prompt a number of relevant observations. First, among the bureaucratic areas with the most reported cases, agriculture and police stand out for the total lack of social organizations that might balance the power of these state organs. The peasant or weak *ejido* worker is commonly fraudulently exploited by members of the agriculture bureaucracies. The prevalence of land fraud reported in Table

3.1 also relates to this form of political exploitation. Despite the existence of peasant organizations, they are not highly developed, are generally controlled from above through co-optation, lack autonomy, and thus offer few checks on the power of the agricultural bureaucracies. The power of the police similarly tends to go virtually unchecked in most parts of the country.

In addition to the high figures for police and agriculture, the incidence of cases is also high for state and local governments. To a certain extent this was not anticipated because of the relative weakness of these governments vis-à-vis the federal government. Yet despite their limited control of resources, local organizations are less able than national-level organizations to check the handling of budgets and programs by local governments.

On the other end of the scale, certain areas with limited cases of corruption are instructive. The low ranking of Congress, for example, reflects its lack of decision-making power and noninvolvement in policy implementation. The low number of cases involving the Mexican military may mirror the relatively high levels of professionalism and the absence of high turnover rates in that corporate body or its ability to shroud corruption behind the walls of national security. The military has increasingly become implicated in drug-related cases of bribery. Finally, as expected, it appears that some of the areas with the highest levels of social organizational strength score somewhat lower in total number of cases. Specifically, banking and industry and commerce, despite their potential for corruption, exhibit a lower number of cases. According to Alan Riding, in the Bank of Mexico and the Finance Ministry "something of a career civil service exists."[54]

A review of the major scandals in the recent past provides further support to these basic patterns. Scandals involve multiple news reports, interrelated cases, or glamorous events or personalities.[55] Most of the more publicized cases of corruption have involved extortion or fraud on the part of high-level government officials rather than large-scale bribery schemes between business and government, including scandals involving fraud on the part of state governors,[56] the national development bank NAFINSA in 1976, the social security institute (IMSS) in 1977,[57] the head of a major government trust (the case of Ríos Camarena at the Bahia de Banderas Trust in 1977),[58] the head of the Secretariat of Agrarian Reform (the Barra García scandal in 1977),[59] officials at the state coffee firm INMECAFE in 1978,[60] numerous wrongdoings in PEMEX and the police, the capture of powerful petroleum union leaders in 1989,[61] and the López Portillo scandal of 1983.[62] Major scandals falling within the bribery category include tax evasion scandals in 1977, 1980, and 1989 (the government claims that "70% of companies do not pay their taxes"),[63] a bribery case involving a judge from Zacatecas,[64] most of the drug-related police scandals, and the Legoretta case.[65] The scandals—involving PEMEX, the STPRM petroleum labor union, the agrarian reform sector, governorships, the police, and even the presidency—normally involved high-level officials occupying political posts rather than highly technocratic positions.

A final hypothesis suggests that strong social organizations inhibit corruption, partly by exposing and denouncing corrupt acts, thereby increasing the likelihood of detection and thus the expected costs of corrupt participation. The data on denouncing parties, however, are difficult to interpret on this point because such a situation would also mean fewer cases of corruption to denounce. In fact, the more autonomous organizations in Mexico, business and professional associations, unexpectedly produced fewer denouncements than unions and peasant groups. Still, most denunciations originated from the government agencies charged with enforcing the Law of Responsibilities: the Justice Department, the Controlaría (Comptroller, formed in 1983), and the police. This may signify these agencies' ability to inculcate strong professional norms to combat corruption and their unique ability (as compared to social organizations) to denounce corruption without retribution. Their strong role in detecting corruption may, however, denote the government's reactionary posture in dealing with the problem.

In sum, the data provide some initial empirical support for the state-society theory linking a particular pattern of corruption to the structural constellation of state and social forces. Here, the analysis of the state-society equation flows from a historical perspective. In Chapter 7, a more dynamic approach is taken, exploring the multifaceted changes that have shaken Mexico during the decade of the 1980s.

4

The Consequences of Corruption in Mexico
Stability and Legitimacy

The second major theoretical issue to be addressed concerns the effects of corruption in Mexico. This analysis of the consequences or functions of corruption hinges on the dialectic between the capacity of corruption to serve as a source of spoils among the elite, on one hand, and its negation of principles of conduct set out by the legitimizing ideology, on the other. From the perspective of the state, this corresponds to the breach between informal organizational procedures that foment the stability of the organizational components of the state and formal procedures that reflect popular legitimacy: though corruption may provide a pragmatic, co-optative device to gain political support crucial to the survival of the system, it is nonetheless inconsistent with the indivisible and uncompromising values of the legitimizing ideology. If corruption involves behavior inconsistent with the state's legitimizing ideology, then to what degree does corruption erode the legitimacy of the government or its personnel? If corruption provides a vehicle for the illegitimate enrichment of a group of elites, then how can this group continue to draw its authority from a state legitimized on contrary principles of conduct?

Corruption and Stability

Previous chapters have stressed the ubiquity of personalist politics in Mexico. This somewhat furtive dimension of the Mexican polity, generally restricted to a rather small group of elites, includes the pervasive practice of patron-clientelism, political teams and middlemen, particularistic contacts and demands, and, of course, corruption. At this level, corruption plays the critical role of integrating these actors and accommodating their demands; it thus facilitates co-optation of the elite and even members of the rising middle class by creating a variety of co-optative mechanisms, including the distribution of spoils, the flexible implementation of public policy, the facilitation of social mobility, and the crippling of threatening mass-based organizations.

Corruption helps bolster feelings of legitimacy among the political elite by offering material benefits to those who play the political game.[1] The impressive opportunities for personal enrichment represented by political appointment (although not the only means to wealth, certainly a major one) aids in maintaining political support and acquiescence among a diverse set of actors; it helps guarantee that participants play by the rules of the game and not disrupt it.[2] According to the Purcells, it helps prevent intraelite conflict.[3]

The use of corruption to integrate an elite and stabilize the system by "buying" support was crucial in the historical development of Mexico's stable regime. Knight, for instance, found that "graft offered the central government a means of buying off generals that was cheap and convenient" during the immediate postrevolutionary period.[4] Students of the Mexican military similarly underscore the role of corruption in gradually removing the military from politics, institutionalizing civilian control, and curbing the divisiveness of regionalism.[5]

Corruption further aids in buying off potential opponents and tempering conflict by making the implementation of public policy more flexible, pragmatic, and accommodating to particularistic demands. On a macro level, corruption allows certain actors a means of escaping the constraints of policies that may not be in their best interest.[6] The illegal disposal of dangerous waste at a major Mexican factory through bribery, noted by one business official, serves as a de facto means of overcoming a costly procedure. The facile bribing of inspectors likewise tends to soften the impact of nominally stringent and otherwise costly environmental controls. Alteration of policy at the implementation stage thereby becomes a means of silently accommodating business interests.

By permitting this variant of hidden or behind-the-scenes influence, corruption thus allows nonideologically sanctioned actors an extralegal means of influencing public policy at the more secretive implementation stage.[7] This is particularly important in the Mexican setting because business does not enjoy (or suffer) official inclusion in the PRI party structure or receive much respect in the official ideology; therefore, it must articulate its demands through personal and particularistic contacts (often accompanied by corrupt or questionable practices) with the Mexican bureaucracy. By mitigating the demands of official legislation or regulations at the implementation stage through bribery, business can shape in some small way the immediate impact of public policy without changing the policy itself. This modus operandi appears to be the norm. As Grindle points out, "Much of the accommodation with business takes place at the implementation stage. As one informant stated, 'The private sector gets along by coming to private and individual terms with the government.'"[8]

The widespread abuse of the *amparo* to block land reform measures provides yet another example of this decentralized, accommodating system. Frequently, the landed elite bribe judges into granting the legal injunction, thereby deflecting the impact of land reform legislation. In 1979, for instance, a subsecretary of the Secretariat of Agrarian Reform assailed this practice, noting the need to "moralize justice in the countryside [so that] the *amparo* would no longer be a form of corruption and legal evasion." The official added that "the corruption of judges" has resulted in more than "five thousand agrarian *amparos* without legal basis."[9]

Corruption-induced policy flexibility helps facilitate personalistic demands, thereby accommodating certain middle-class wishes for mobility as well. Although generally the rewards of corruption accrue to the governing elite, members of the Mexican middle class often resort to corruption to "arrange" a bureaucratic problem, "buy" immunity from criminal prosecution, or "purchase" a college degree or a well-paying government job. Indeed, for many members of the Mexican middle class, corruption has at one time or another resolved a serious dilemma. This form of co-optation bolsters an individual's stake in the stability and maintenance of the system.

Finally, corruption functions at this intricate personalistic level to stabilize the system by discouraging horizontal mobilization of classes or occupational groups.[10] This occurs in two ways. First, corruption adds to the potential to co-opt leaders of potentially powerful and threatening horizontal groups (such as labor unions) into supporting the position of the government. It is common practice in Mexico to "allow" powerful labor leaders the opportunity to exploit their own organizations and enjoy other special privileges from the regime in return for their support in controlling the demands of labor. The sale of *plazas* (jobs) by union leaders and sweetheart contracts amply illustrate this lucrative corporatist arrangement.[11] The outcome has been a docile and relatively tame labor movement.

Second, the alternative offered by corruption makes it easier to channel political demands through the system in a personal fashion at the implementation stage rather than through broad-based pressures at the policy-making stage.[12] Corruption, as one observer notes, "discourages mobilization because its logic and incentives emphasize the divisible over the shared, the tangible over the intangible and the immediate over the long term."[13] It thus avoids the more destabilizing demands of groups or classes by rewarding those who pursue their demands on a particularistic level.

In contrast to the use of opposition parties or interest associations, channeling demands through the personalistic network appears quite effective in most cases. After registering negative responses on government performance generally, for example, one survey found that 90 percent of those who personally contacted public officials received good treatment and two-thirds said that such personal contact was beneficial.[14] As they are in business, such styles of political negotiation and bargaining seem to be common practice throughout the country.

In sum, corruption promotes political stability, particularly among the elite, through its integrative tendencies. It encourages political pragmatism and helps the elite escape the rough edges of public policies by altering their implementation. Basically, corruption facilitates the co-optation of political support.

Inefficiency and Mismanagement: The Other Side of the Coin

Although corruption produces spoils for the elite and thus accommodates particularistic demands, the other side of the coin is bureaucratic inefficiency, waste, and the undermining of legitimate social programs. Public funds are diverted by and to participants in the elite game, rewarding those already served by the system for their continued support and undermining legitimate policy objectives. According to Kenneth Johnson, corruption thus "defeats whatever quests there may be in Mexico for concrete government reforms," a clue perhaps, he suggests, as to "why countries like Mexico seem to be always 'developing' but somehow never really develop."[15]

Examples of waste and inefficiency in the Mexican bureaucracy abound. The postal service, for instance, estimated its 1979 losses at 400 million pesos (approximately U.S. $16 million) through the fraudulent sale of fifteen hundred *franquicias* (franking privileges);[16] in Nuevo Laredo, according to an opposition party, a full three-quarters of the 1982 budget fell victim to corruption;[17] and a British consultant estimated a leakage of 15 percent of the $1 billion cost associated with the Las Truchas steel complex to corruption.[18]

Not only are funds pilfered through corruption taken from already struggling social programs, thus undermining their effectiveness, but resources are also squandered through the creation of complicated corrupt schemes and procedures. Costly subcontracting or the purchase of land by government officials who then resell to the government for public works contracts are good examples. This practice operates as a multiplier effect on the diversion of resources from corruption. "The problem with corruption," argues one official, "is that a hundred pesos may be spent unnecessarily in order to steal ten pesos."[19] These few cases stand for the many that could be recounted.

Corruption, Society, and Legitimacy

Corruption functions to stabilize the political game by rewarding obedient participants, but serious questions arise as to its impact on society at large, particularly the state's popular legitimacy. It would seem that corruption, as a negation of the principles of the legitimizing ideology, combined with bureaucratic inefficiency and ineffective social programs, would totally delegitimize the system, prompting protest, popular mobilization, and instability.

Perhaps the most pernicious effect of corruption on the public at large has been to foster a generalized "culture of corruption" or "folklore of corruption" in Mexico.[20] According to Victor Le Vine, such a culture exists when "politically corrupt transactions become so pervasive in a political system that they are the expected norm;"[21] a characterization that surely applies to Mexico. When asked how often it is necessary to pay a bribe when dealing with the government, for example, 40.4 percent of the respondents said "always" and another 38.3 percent indicated that it was required "much of the time" (see Chapter 6 for a discussion of the 1986 survey).

The Mexican culture of corruption is characterized by the proliferation of corruption throughout civil society, the cultural glorification of corruption among certain sectors of the population, the engendering of a distorted middle-class morality, diversion of individual responsibility, and the diffusion of distrust and cynicism toward the government and public officials. It is this pervasive culture of corruption that creates the social inertia that renders difficult efforts at curbing corruption.

Corruption invades virtually all dimensions of social life, producing what Simeha Werner refers to as a "spillover effect." In Mexico, corruption extends into nongovernmental areas such as business, private education, and even the church. Tannenbaum long ago identified this diffusion: "This blight [the *mordida*] has spread from public officeholders to inspectors, to clerks, and from them to petty labor leaders and even to private employees." Enrique Florescano echoes the point: "Since the government of Miguel Aleman, corruption invaded other sectors of national life such as . . . the centers of higher education . . . it is a general phenomenon in the public and private sectors."[22]

Again examples of corruption in civil society abound. Not only does corruption pervade education, as Florescano suggests (note the high number of cases in Table 3.2), but according to the archbishop in Hermosillo, even the church is tainted by corruption.[23] In the private sector, likewise, tax fraud and evasion are particularly widespread as are the practices of speculative hoarding and overpricing.[24] One official in Jalisco, for example, claimed that 97 percent of businesses fail to pay their taxes.[25] One incredible case in the private sector involved a medical school in the state of Chihuahua illegally extracting and fraudulently selling retinas and corneas, a practice that was said to have extended over a three-year period.[26]

Moreover, the Mexican culture of corruption exhibits a subcultural acceptance or glorification of corruption. Just as corrupt gains made at the expense of foreigners carry a certain propriety and nationalistic pride, it often appears that those making illicit gains exhibit a certain immodesty in their accomplishments and are seemingly the target of admiration. Plays, movies, and even comic books depicting the corrupt maneuvers of police chief Arturo Durazo, for example, enjoyed wide appeal in Mexico in the mid-1980s. Despite the contemptuous and illegal nature of Durazo's activities, the man projected a certain "heroized" aura.

This glorification of corruption is detected most brazenly in the accounts provided by rising young bureaucrats or politicians, who often exalt their "commissions," their mysterious earnings, and their "rapid mobility." Manuel Buendía detected a similar phenomenon within the private sector, pointing out that businessmen caught for tax fraud are often treated as heroes of the "high society."[27] Combined with the frequent use of corrupt means to obtain individual benefits, the models of "success" have led, according to one observer, to "a new middle-class morality" in Mexico in which corruption constitutes a dependable and prominent tool for social advancement.[28]

This subcultural glorification of corruption may stem in part from Mexican *machismo*. Brilliantly portrayed by Octavio Paz in his classic treatment of the Mexican culture, *machismo* contemplates a deep-seated dichotomy of prowess versus weakness, of either inflicting violent action or suffering its consequences.[29] From this vantage point, an individual partaking of corrupt gains projects a romantic image of the unrestrained and the unconquered. This *machismo* and the glorification of corruption that go with it may, however, simply reflect the structural conditions of poverty and underdevelopment. In a sense, the realities of poverty bring a certain disdain to moral and ethical considerations that try further to inhibit economic opportunities. The young bureaucrat enjoying mobility often escapes the injustice which his or her family may have suffered for years; individual participation in corruption is easily justified subjectively.

Underlying this culture of corruption stands the diversion of individual responsibility. As Romanucci-Ross expresses it: "Individual responsibility is submerged in the notion that everyone will steal given the opportunity."[30] This interpretation of human nature indeed seems to flourish in the minds of many. Such a worldview not only helps justify and excuse one's participation in corrupt activities, it clearly helps perpetuate the practice. Public officials who patiently and obediently await the opportunity to partake of the system's spoils often consider it their right to do so, while members of society rely on corruption to compete for mobility.

Politically, the culture of corruption translates into widespread cynicism and popular distrust of government and public officials.[31] As one businessman unequivocally asserts, "We Mexicans are very cynical and we doubt our Government and expect the worse from it. . . . We are ready to believe that every government employee is a thief."[32] Consequently, "political authority as such is discredited."[33] This distrust results not only from widespread corruption but also from the related inefficiencies and waste of government funds.

Survey research on Mexico has often confirmed this pervasive cynicism and distrust among the population. Gabriel Almond and Sidney Verba, for example, found that more than

50 percent of those polled did not expect fair treatment from the government or the police. They quoted one small businessman as saying that "in the local government, they will do their duty for money."[34] Results of the opinion poll conducted in 1986, to be discussed in Chapter 6, also revealed this high degree of distrust.

Defusing Distrust: Corruption and the Accountability Factor

Clearly, distrust, cynicism, and the related inefficiencies fostered by widespread corruption pose potentially destabilizing and devastating consequences; they seriously compromise and erode the legitimacy of the system. But historically, this has not been the case because for alienation and distrust to undermine legitimacy, they must be targeted and linked to the system itself. And yet the state's ability to manipulate the normative dimension of corruption makes it difficult to draw this linkage.

The normative meaning of corruption (as something "bad") is a unique political phenomenon that lends itself to displacing blame for social or government problems and assigning culpability to less destabilizing targets. This occurs in a variety of ways. First, corruption is widely perceived and touted as a personalistic rather than a systemic problem. Emphasis on the unsavory outcome of "a few bad apples" deflects public attention away from broader and perhaps more divisive problems relating to the system. One leader of the PRI stressed this interpretation: "When a candidate of the party fails, this failure should be attributed to the man himself, who is susceptible to being mistaken; it should not be attributed to the Party, nor to its doctrine, nor to its program."[35]

A review of the news articles on corruption discussed in the previous chapter tends to support this personalistic interpretation of corruption. By a margin of roughly two to one, the articles portray corruption as stemming from personal inadequacies rather than systemic ones. Few highlight systemic causes for corruption or discuss system-related changes; rather, they generally emphasize the corruption of the individual, the solitary act, and the atomistic punishment of malfeasance.

A similar shift in accountability concerns the use of corruption as a scapegoat device to explain the existence or persistence of social or political problems. Blaming corruption for social problems implies that if politicians were honest, the problems could be resolved.[36] Thus important ideological conflict is defused by reducing systemic issues or questions of policy into matters regarding idiosyncratic behavior; issues of structure and policy are turned into problems of personnel, procedures, and recruitment. Highlighting the problem of a few bad apples, the governor of Guanajuato suggested that "traitors within the PRI produced political sabotage . . . with which they intend to devour the force of their own party." Such officials, he added, would henceforth be excluded from the party.[37] A member of Congress similarly assailed the corrupt officials in the agricultural sector for "treason against President Miguel de la Madrid for not achieving the objectives of his agricultural policy."[38]

Finally, in addition to diverting attention away from more systemic issues, corruption is also used rhetorically in an effort to disassociate one *sexenio* from another, the party from the government, or simply the "good guys" from the "bad guys." Reflecting the important distinction between party and government, a PRI official once incredibly claimed that the PRI is not responsible for corrupt government officials.[39] The powerful labor czar Fidel Velázquez provides an even more poignant example; he stated categorically that "there are no corrupt individuals in the PRI. Those who were members and are found guilty of wrongdoing, are automatically removed."[40]

Using corruption to disassociate the incoming administration from its predecessor by attacking the corruption of the prior regime has often been a salient political tactic. Despite similar pundits and tax evasion scandals in the past, for instance, the arrest of financial giant Eduardo Legorretta in 1989 "has been interpreted as a clear warning by the government . . . that fiscal law will now be strictly enforced."[41] Another example of disassociation comes from a PRI senator, who in 1976 publicly stated that in contrast to the corruption of the Echeverría period, posts in the new administration of López Portillo would be filled by the best men.[42] Yet in attacking this common practice, an editorialist later asserted: "It is sad that all these scandals are only uncovered now . . . they should have appeared in that period when Mr. Echeverría was still in the government . . . with the responsibility as chief executive."[43] This indictment of the system would later be voiced most resoundingly against Echeverría's successor and later against his successor's successor.

The anticorruption campaign is the institutionalized vehicle for disassociating one administration from another and generally sustaining these images of corruption (aspects of certain anticorruption campaigns are discussed in Chapter 5). Typically, the campaign stresses the view that the "bad apples" of the prior period have been rooted out and that, contrary to the past, the current administration is (finally) serious in pursuing much-needed reforms, including the eradication of corruption. Generally, an anticorruption campaign underscores virtually all the dimensions of the accountability factor noted above. Not only do such campaigns socialize the public into viewing a systemic problem as an individual problem, but they also serve an important mobilizing and ritualistic function by ceremonially "rooting the society of evil," thus striving to rejuvenate popular faith in the moral integrity of public office,[44] sustaining and reaffirming support for the goals of the Mexican Revolution, and decrying the corrupt officials who have thwarted their attainment. In this sense, attacking corruption becomes a crucial facet in the expression of patriotic fervor and hence an important mobilizational tool of the government.

This ritualistic, symbolic use of corruption through the anticorruption drive, moreover, assists the government in filling the accountability vacuum created by the shifting of blame by targeting public frustrations toward individuals culpable of political heresy (corruption). The intense and spectacular media hype surrounding the scandalous cases of police chief Arturo Durazo or Jorge Díaz Serrano of PEMEX during De la Madrid's Moral Renovation campaign, for example, demonstrated the nature of this public rite. Durazo's luxurious estate was placed on public exhibition temporarily by the government as a "museum of corruption." Truly awe-inspiring, the museum served as a clear demonstration not of a corrupt system of government but of the government's firm commitment to struggle on behalf of the Mexican people to thwart the avaricious tendencies of such individuals. It was clearly a monument designed to enhance the state's legitimacy.

Such symbolic manipulation has been employed frequently by the Mexican government. In fact, most Mexican presidents have pinpointed corruption as a major problem plaguing Mexican society and have vowed to root it out. President Calles's efforts to "uplift the moral level of the people," for example, were important "in that they formed a key element of the Constitutionalist ethos and claimed a great deal of political time and attention."[45] President Manuel Avila Camacho (1940–46) promised in 1940 to foster "stronger public morals." Widespread corruption during the term of Alemán in the late 1940s and early 1950s led his successor, Adolfo Ruiz Cortines, to institute a series of reforms, including requiring public officials to submit financial statements upon taking office and again on leaving.[46] In more recent times, virtually every administration has boasted some form of anticorruption campaign.

In sum, through frequent anticorruption movements, the government socializes the public into viewing corruption as an individual problem of certain officials rather than as a systemic problem. Incoming administrations then promote the view that the personnel problems of the past have been resolved. The result is to separate feelings toward public officials from overall evaluations of the system. Even protests against corruption or corrupt officials become less destabilizing because the government does not defend the corruption as it would an "official" policy. In fact, the government leads the assault on corruption and thus sides with the public on the issue. With strong rhetoric, the government emphasizes its cooperation with the public on the matter, giving the appearance of being responsive to popular demands.

Corruption and Change

Central to understanding its linkage to stability is the paradox of corruption and change. The logic of corruption encapsulates its capacity to promote the status quo by altering government programs and rewarding important government clients (the elite), yet simultaneously allowing the government to respond to popular demands through the development of popularly supported policy (including demands for an end to corruption). The government therefore gives the appearance of promoting change while undermining it. In other words, government is afforded the luxury of changing nothing while giving the solemn appearance of promoting change.

Moreover, corruption provides a convenient tool for assigning blame for persistent failures at achieving change. Individual scapegoats or, more generally, the natural avarice of human nature are depicted as the cause of corruption in Mexico, not the system. The government therefore sides with those decrying corruption and its own inability to achieve its announced goals, inviting their cooperation in eliminating this nonsystemic problem. The enticements of corrupt spoils can be relied upon to quell the dissent of those in society who rise above the alienation to attack the system. For most, however, the end result is to divert attention away from destabilizing issues or problems and to cripple or tame opposition to the system. In Mexico, these consequences have long interacted to contribute to a remarkable record of political stability.

Thus corruption has fostered a paradoxical system wherein the regime, in support of its "revolutionary" credentials, responds to popular pressures by making popular public policy (centralized in the hands of the executive), which in the end does not threaten the elite or truly alter the essential functioning of the stable, decentralized, personalistic system. While the government promotes the status quo and rewards the elite for its acquiesence, at the same time it condemns, combats, and curses corruption in the public forum. Mobilizing the public in the anticorruption fight, the regime thus reaffirms its support for the goals of the revolution and co-opts popular opposition. Without it, many of the divisive contradictions of the system would be fully exposed.

Two Conditions for the Relationship

Corruption's contribution to stability is conditioned on two important factors: maintaining corruption within certain limits and the existence of abundant resources. First, limits must be maintained so as to retain some degree of centralized control; otherwise the system would disintegrate. This task is accomplished largely through manipulation of the normative dimension of corruption (as something "bad") as a "scarlet letter" tactic to purge government officials who have either lost political favor or excessively abused their privileges.[47] The threat of being exposed, prosecuted, and deposed for corruption is ever-present in the minds of bureaucrats and hence places an upper limit on their corrupt gains and other political activities.

As one official noted: "There is a Law of Responsibility of Public Officials which we are all aware can be applied. Clearly, it isn't applied very rigidly now, but I think in this *sexenio* the President [Echeverría] has made very clear to what point he is willing to tolerate deviant or dishonest behavior from public officials."[48]

Using this device to enforce informal rules within the state and ensure loyalty is common, although difficult to prove. Raúl Olmedo notes, for example, that "the accusation of corruption has other ends than to terminate with corruption. It is simply the utilization of a political weapon against someone who is to be politically destroyed."[49] Indeed, there is evidence to support this conclusion. Riding contends that the strategy was widely employed during the Echeverría administration, and accusations linger that the cases against Eugenio Méndez Docurro, and Cantú Peña were politically motivated.[50] Even the "glorious" case of Jorge Díaz Serrano of PEMEX raised suspicions, particularly since Díaz Serrano was once considered a likely successor to López Portillo and thus a competitor against the man who orchestrated his fall. One editorial focusing on the case provocatively questioned why it was that "so many other far more obvious culprits have slipped away," including López Portillo.[51] Indeed, since "corruption is to such an extent an integral part of the system, to limit the application of justice only to . . . [one individual] has little value."[52] It is equally common for those who "slip away" to be close friends and those brought down to be political enemies. It is well known that some of the more important victims of the Salinas anticorruption drive belonged to labor unions that openly opposed his nomination.

The second condition required for the stable functioning of corruption is the abundant availability of resources. Generally, this means economic growth; specifically, it encompasses copious state-controlled resources as a source of spoils. The importance of this factor can be seen at both the levels of the elite and the general public.

For the elite, an abundant and perhaps even growing resource base is needed to maintain the accommodation game. A situation of scarce or dwindling resources available to co-opt key actors incites and engenders greater elite competition for the rewards and has a tendency to divide rather than unite the elite. Rooted in assimilation and co-optation, as Howard J. Wiarda contends, the system "requires a constantly expanding economic pie so that new 'pieces' can be handed out to the rising groups without the old ones being deprived."[53]

Among the public, bountiful resources are important in corruption's relationship to stability in two crucial ways. First, they support the system's capacity to respond to particularistic demands and accommodate avenues of social mobility. Thus during periods of economic growth, the public (particularly the middle class) can partake in some of the perceived benefits of corruption. Second, the public's threshold of acceptability of corruption tends to be high during prosperous economic periods. In other words, the excesses of the political elite are more permissible when certain elements of society are also enjoying the fruits of the system. When the government is at least delivering on its promise of economic growth, corruption is seen as an affordable aberration or nuisance. But when resources grow scant, once acceptable levels of corruption can suddenly become a source of alienation and political protest.

Clearly, these conditions have obtained virtually throughout the postrevolutionary history of Mexico. Until 1982, the record of economic growth was solid, particularly during the 1940–70 period, touted as the "Mexican Miracle," when gross domestic product averaged a yearly increase of 6 percent and the proportion of resources controlled by the state steadily increased. A degree of centralized control over the political elite was maintained and corruption seemingly remained within limits throughout the period.

Questions arise, however, as to whether such conditions have prevailed since 1982. Economic growth and the resources mobilized by the state have declined, and, some feel, corruption has overstepped its boundaries. This suggests not only that the functions of corruption and its linkage to stability may be undergoing change but that the state-society balance may be shifting. These questions, centering on the dynamics of corruption in Mexico, are taken up in Chapter 7.

5 Corruption and the *Sexenio*
Patterns of Corruption and the Anticorruption Campaign

Mexican politics revolves around the *sexenio*, the six-year presidential term. Dynamics of government spending, bureaucratic conduct, and public policy stem largely from this political cycle, as does corruption. Bringing together the earlier analyses of cause and consequence, this chapter explores the short-term patterns of corruption in Mexico and the nature of the anticorruption campaign.

Sexenial Patterns

Given the power of the Mexican president, the absence of a civil service system and reelections, and the high turnover rate in government, the transition from one presidential administration to another represents a decisive shift.[1] The initial year is a "get-acquainted" period in which the new government focuses its energies on filling the numerous bureaucratic posts in its empire and designing new programs and policies; individual bureaucracts spend time familiarizing themselves with their new surroundings, responsibilities, and clients. During the second year, the president and his top officials take control, enthusiastically implementing and promoting comprehensive government programs and reforms. This posture generally holds throughout the middle years of the term.

During the fifth year of the *sexenio*, Mexican politics exhibits discernible changes. No new programs or reforms are inaugurated, but established programs receive a concerted impetus with increased spending and the personal attention and support of bureaucratic leaders trying to leave a personal legacy on their bureaucratic agencies. Most important though, in the final years officials set their sights on the approaching political transition. Particularly during the sixth and final year of the term, government officials concentrate their efforts on enhancing their prospects for political appointment in the next term or securing economic security in the event that they have to leave public service. Officials consolidate their political support groups, praise the accomplishments of the outgoing administration, publicly articulate the standard revolutionary language, and strategically avoid public controversy. Presidential hopefuls, meanwhile, solidify their support among the upper elite and, without appearing to campaign, meticulously vie for the outgoing president's attention and favor. The subsequent electoral confirmation of the PRI presidential candidate, hand-picked by the outgoing chief executive, caps a massive nationwide campaign that seeks to replenish faith in the Mexican Revolution, the PRI, and the incoming president. When the new chief executive takes office, the six-year pattern begins anew.

The major causes of corruption and the anticorruption campaign discussed earlier interact during the course of a presidential term to forge a discernible pattern. First, a conflueuce of factors conspires to enhance the prospects and opportunities for corruption during the final years of an administrative term. High turnover rates, the lack of job security, and the absence of a solid pension or retirement fund often lead public officials to prepare individual retirement schemes; even for those who continue in government, the unlikelihood of remaining at their current post erodes their accountability to the constituents of the agency. Increased public spending and a weakening of the anticorruption campaign during the latter years of the term further contribute to the opportunities for corruption. The result is widespread corruption during the final year of the *sexenio*. It is so widespread, in fact, that the year is popularly dubbed the "year of Hidalgo" (referring to Miguel Hidalgo's likeness on Mexican currency): "este es el ano de Hidalgo, chin-chin el que deje algo" ("this is the 'year of Hidalgo', he is a fool [polite form] who leaves something").

A second set of factors operates to depress the level of corruption during the initial years of the *sexenio*. On the heels of the upbeat presidential campaign, officials tend to wax enthusiastic about their new posts, the new president, and the prospects for contributing positively to the Mexican Revolution during the initial years. Because of the high turnover rate and reshuffling, they are generally unfamiliar with their new bureaucratic surroundings and responsibilities, making it more difficult to elaborate complicated schemes to defraud the agency or its clients; besides, most are relatively secure in their posts for a time and do not feel any pressure to "get what they can" at this stage. The fear of detection is greater anyway during the early years of the *sexenio* because of the heightened controls and sensitivities stemming from the anticorruption campaign.

A key feature of the *sexenial* pattern is the anticorruption campaign, which fulfills a host of important social and political functions corresponding to the initial years of the *sexenio*: it helps the incoming administration disassociate itself from the previous administration; it diverts attention from certain issues and problems; it attempts to boost the legitimacy of the new government among the popular sectors; it allows a means of purging political enemies; and it foments centralized, presidential control over a virtually new crop of bureaucratic officials. Because these functions are carried out during the initial years, the anticorruption campaign is most pronounced and effective at reinforcing the tendency for lowered incidence of corruption during this time. As the term wears on, however, the crusade's steam dissipates: the rhetoric fades, fewer scandals of corruption emerge, and confidence and enthusiasm erode within the bureaucratic ranks. The waning years of the López Portillo administration, for example, found "the official war against the venality of public officials which, at the beginning of the *sexenio,* seemed to have great enthusiasm, has been lost in lethargy, technicalities and virtual cover-ups."[2] As one authority explained the similar fate of De la Madrid's campaign, the initial measures to fight corruption eventually become counterproductive.[3] Either way, such diminishing currents crystallize precisely at a time when the opportunities for corruption billow.

In sum, the *sexenio* produces a pattern composed of two major ingredients: the year of Hidalgo and the anticorruption campaign. Figure 5.1 graphically illustrates this hypothesized relationship. It shows corruption gradually increasing as the term unfolds, crowned by extensive corruption during the year of Hidalgo (the final year of the *sexenio*). The transition to a new regime, however, brings a marked decline in the level of corruption, in tandem with the emergence of an anticorruption campaign. As the period wears on, the force of the anticorruption sentiment erodes and the level of corruption gradually picks up once again.

Although analytically distinct, the year of Hidalgo and the anticorruption campaign represent two sides of the same coin. That is, the excesses of public officials during the year of Hidalgo create the objective necessity for the subsequent campaign—a reaction designed to curb the abuses, reinstitute control over public officials, channel popular outcries against corruption, and generally boost the legitimacy of the new regime. The anticorruption campaign plays a major role in exposing the abuses of the year of Hidalgo and fostering the general

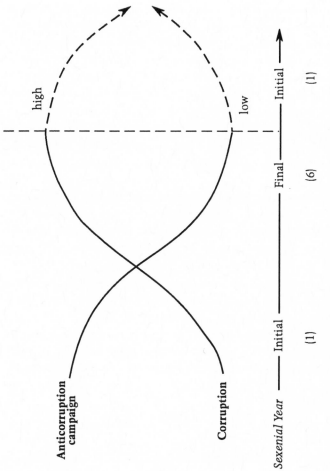

Figure 5.1. Sexenial Patterns of Corruption and Anticorruption Campaigns

verdict of the previous anticorruption drive. The popular image of the year of Hidalgo is therefore in part a product of the anticorruption campaign.

Data from news articles on corruption lend support to these conclusions. Figure 5.2 and Table 5.1 classify reports by type and year to show the number of corruption-related stories during three *sexenios*. The data clearly show more corruption-related stories during the first years of the three presidential terms (1971, 1977, and 1983) than during any of the other years. The surge in the number of reports includes both substantial increases in the number of cases reported (reflecting the abuses of the year of Hidalgo) and general denouncements and promises of anticorruption reforms (reflecting the anticorruption campaign). Since not all of these reports come from government sources, the data underscore the role of the public in the periodic outcry against corruption every six years.

This basic pattern seems to apply somewhat loosely to other *sexenios* in Mexico relating to state governments, although these *sexenios* do not run concurrent with those of the federal government. Incoming state governors often ignite anticorruption movements in their states during the initial year of their term, frequently exposing the corruption of the previous administration. The governor of Yucatán, for example, strongly pushed the anticorruption theme after taking office in 1978, as did the governor of Hidalgo.[4] Still, state officials are more often attacked or exposed for wrongdoing by federal officials than by state officials.

The Anticorruption Campaign

The workings of the anticorruption campaign are important in understanding the role of corruption in Mexico and its linkage to the *sexenio*. An analysis of the anticorruption campaigns directed by Presidents Echeverría, López Portillo, and

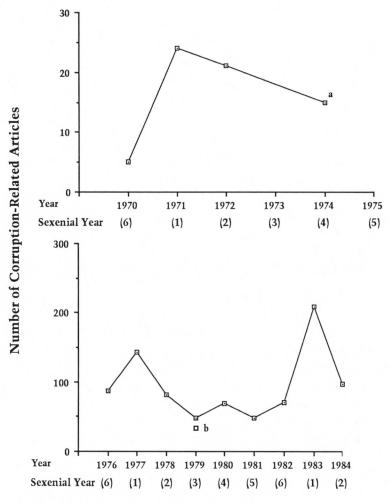

[a] Only a random sample of fifty-two newpapers per year was reviewed for the years 1970, 1971, 1972, and 1974. The numbers are therefore not comparable with those from other years, which reflect a more exhaustive research.

[b] The 1979 figure is based on a review of only nine months. The figure is thus adjusted to an estimated yearly basis by adding one-third of the number of reports to the total.

Figure 5.2. Corruption-Related News Articles by Year

Table 5.1. Corruption-Related News Articles by Year

Year and Year of Sexenio

Category	1970 (6)	1971 (1)	1972 (2)	1974 (4)
Cases	1	17	10	10
General denunciations	1	5	7	4
Reforms	3	2	4	1
Total	5	24	21	15

Category	1976 (6)	1977 (1)	1978 (2)	1979# (3)	1980 (4)	1981 (5)	1982 (6)
Cases	63	80	56	22	48	36	47
General denunciations	11	34	13	5	9	6	12
Reforms	13	29	12	8	12	6	11
Total	87	143	81	35(47)	69	48	70

Category	1983 (1)	1984 (2)
Cases	139	77
General denunciations	38	12
Reforms	32	8
Total	209	97

#Based on review of nine months. The figure in parentheses is an adjusted total calculated by adding an additional one-third of the nine-month total.

De la Madrid and initial impressions of Salinas's strikes against corruption reveal three basic similarities. First, the anticorruption campaign includes three essential components: rhetoric and mobilization, the prosecution of public officials, and structural and legal reforms. Second, anticorruption campaigns carry certain inherent dangers, such as how to deal with former presidents, that often detract from their credibility. Third, despite the serious tone they project and the optimism they inspire, anticorruption campaigns have proved largely unsuccessful in more than temporarily curbing the incidence of corruption.

The first element of the anticorruption campaign involves political rhetoric against corruption and promises for reform. This usually begins during the presidential campaign and continues at particularly high levels during the initial years of the administration. Soon after his designation as the ruling party's candiate, for example, López Portillo denounced corruption in specific areas such as CONASUPO (state-owned agricultural distribution firm), the Secretariat of Agrarian Reform (SRA), and the Secretariat of Hydraulic Resources (SRH) and lashed out at corruption in speeches at Atoyac de Alvarez and Chilpancingo, in the state of Mexico. Later in his campaign, he called for the complete reorganization of the judicial system. Upon taking office, he assailed the poor administration of state industries and urged public disclosures of their financial records.[5]

De la Madrid similarly criticized corruption during his campaign and even attacked earlier anticorruption efforts as demagoguery.[6] Calling for "a new moral revolution," the president promised to introduce "new methods in the public sector to prevent, detect, correct and, in such a case, punish immoral acts of public officials and public employees. . . . You either govern or you conduct business. Public office should not be anyone's spoils."[7]

While presidents set the tone of the anticorruption campaign, others in the government dance to the beat. During the López Portillo campaign, for instance, the Justice Department promised to attack corruption without showing favoritism to millionaires and politicians; the Mexican Confederation of Workers vowed to fight corruption within the federal government; and Congress and opposition parties demanded solid changes to deter corruption such as the registration of properties of public officials. Even officials from the Secretariat of Agrarian Reform and the police (both notoriously corrupt) announced their resolve to cleanse their corruption-riddled agencies.[8]

The rhetoric of the anticorruption campaign encompasses not only attacks on corruption by the political leadership and promises of reform but also efforts to enjoin the public in the fight and to pinpoint the causes of corruption. In June 1977, for example, López Portillo urged peasants to form a common front to eliminate corruption in the agricultural sector;[9] De la Madrid made similar exhortations years later. In delineating cause, Echeverría "stressed the fact that corruption could not exist at the bottom of the bureaucratic chain if it did not exist at the top," and López Portillo held that "immorality" was practiced not by high-level officials but rather by administrative employees.[10] Setting out a third course, De la Madrid later emphasized that "corruption is not solely the domain of the public sector, but of all society."[11]

In addition to the rhetoric, the anticorruption campaign features the persecution and prosecution of public officials for wrongdoing, particularly those of the previous administration. Both highly publicized scandals and lower-level, less public investigations are included in the denunciations. These attacks play an important role in disassociating the new regime from its predecessor and the problems of the past and in harassing political enemies. Although the government denied that it was "organizing a persecution of officials,"[12] a barrage of political scandals (the Félix Barra García scandal, the Alfredo Ríos Camarena scandal, the IMSS scandal, and the tax evasion scandal) flooded the pages of the major newspapers throughout 1977. In the closing days of September, sixteen editorials appeared praising the moves of the government and urging greater action against the corrupt officials of the previous administration.[13] During the De la Madrid period, two major cases attracted worldwide attention: those against the former director of PEMEX, Jorge Díaz Serrano and the former chief of the Mexico City police, Arturo Durazo Moreno. The latter was a close friend of former president López Portillo. Both cases produced major public spectacles. Before their criminal trials, Díaz Serrano had to be stripped of his senatorial immunity and Durazo had to be extradited from Los Angeles.

Although less publicized or scandalous, other prosecutions underlie the campaign. By May 1978, for example, the Justice Department claimed it had investigated 903 public officials and handled a total of 3,000 denunciations of corruption since the *sexenio* began.[14] By October of the following year, the López Portillo administration boasted the prosecution of 759 officials, the investigation of another 1,500, and the recovery of 2 billion pesos. By February 1980, the government claimed to have arrested more than 800 persons for fraud, tax evasion, and similar offenses over a three-year period, recovering a total of 4 billion pesos.[15]

In 1983, the government again bragged of its catch. The Justice Department announced that in the first ten months of the year it had recovered some 11 billion, 200 million pesos from 30 officials jailed for corruption.[16] Meanwhile, the newly created anticorruption agency, the Comptroller General, disclosed that it had conducted 600 audits in 353 departments in 1983 and 700 in 1984.[17] Later, the agency claimed that it had prosecuted 4,500 employees, handled 7,000 complaints and public denouncements from 1983 to 1986, and disclosed for the first time the financial reports of some 50 government-owned firms.[18]

Other agencies besides the Justice Department and Comptroller pursue the prosecution crusade as the mood of the campaign diffuses throughout the bureaucracy.[19] The chief of the Mexico City police, Arturo Durazo, for example, publicized the firing or reassignment of some 3,000 officers in an effort to curb police corruption. A few days later, he stated that he would "achieve the moralization of the police or . . . retire." By September 1979, Durazo claimed to have fired 6,000 police for corruption of which 800 were prosecuted.[20]

In addition to prosecution and rhetoric, the anticorruption campaign features legal-structural reforms designed to curb corruption. Such reforms may be directly or indirectly targeted at corruption. During the López Portillo campaign, for instance, reforms were carried out in three areas. First, López Portillo promoted greater oversight powers among the population and Congress to check corruption. Although his efforts to create greater public oversight resulted in a weak system of "information booths" in government buildings, reforms in the Organic Law of Public Accounting granted the Chamber of Deputies greater power to oversee and sanction the use of public monies by the executive.[21] To enhance legislative power, López Portillo also undertook a political reform that strengthened and increased the representation of opposition parties in the Chamber of Deputies. In that "the political monopoly of the PRI has been a determining factor in corruption," the political opening was expected to help fight corruption.[22]

Second, López Portillo amended the Law of Responsibilities covering public employees to require public officials periodically to register their properties with the Justice Department and to strengthen the legal base for punishing corrupt officials.[23] The Justice Department declared that the changes would also prevent the use of the Law of Responsibilities for purposes of political revenge.[24] According to one observer, the legal changes meant that "the old taboo that high officials of the government enjoy impunity has been broken."[25]

Finally, López Portillo promoted sweeping administrative reforms designed in part to fight corruption. These changes brought about a reorganization and reassignment of government functions, created a new bureaucratic agency charged with coordinating spending and planning (the Secretary of Planning and Budgeting), and enhanced bureaucratic controls and supervision by mandating additional public audits.[26] The underlying premise was "to organize the government so as to organize the country."[27] One official claimed that the administrative reforms of López Portillo had done more to fight corruption than the Penal Code.[28]

Under De la Madrid, additional legal-structural reforms directed specifically at the problem of corruption formed the cornerstone of the president's highly visible Moral Renovation campaign.[29] The term *public officials* in the Título Cuarto Constitutional was amended to read *public servants*, thereby expanding the scope and application of laws pertaining to corruption. The crucial Law of Responsibilities was again changed to establish an extensive Code of Obligations for public officials (Title 3) and require more complete registration of properties of public officials (Title 4). The stipulation was added that failure to declare income or property was tantamount to a presumption of illicit enrichment. Additional reforms in the law limited the value of a gift an official could receive to ten times the daily minimum wage and specifically defined and outlawed nepotism. And the penal code was amended to enhance the state's ability to punish corrupt officials by adding five new categories of offenses, including such crimes as illicit use of public resources, conflict of interest, influence peddling, and illicit enrichment. The juridical definitions of such crimes as abuse of authority, bribery, and extortion also were broadened.

Probably the most crucial structural reform of De la Madrid's campaign involved the creation of a new bureaucratic agency charged with the prevention and policing of corruption: La Secretaría General de la Controlaría de la Federación (SGCF) or Comptroller General. Often referred to as the corruption czar, the Comptroller was established to implement and coordinate the various aspects of the entire campaign. Three subsecretariats within the secretariat were established: one to implement the reformed Law of Responsibilities, a second to conduct audits of government agencies, and a third to set up comptroller commissions within each bureaucratic agency.[30] Of the various activities, one of the more important brought an array of publicly accessible offices for handling complaints and denunciations of corruption.[31]

Other reforms under De la Madrid indirectly impinged on the anticorruption effort. The reorganization of the judicial police forces, including the elimination of the much feared and corrupt Directorate of Investigation for the Prevention of Delinquency special forces (secret police) and greater regulation of the Mexico City police, for example, were undertaken in part to reduce the corruption permeating the police.[32] Similarly, a 1984 program of "administrative simplification" pushed for the elimination of layers of red tape in the Mexican bureaucratic labyrinth to remove much of the opportunity for malfeasance.[33] These changes included the gradual elimination of many licensing arrangements, a frequently abused form of regulating business.

Although the rhetoric, prosecutions, and reforms serve an important political role, the anticorruption campaign carries certain dangers. Two problems are particularly noteworthy. First, an anticorruption campaign strives to rejuvenate faith in the government and must therefore be careful not to trigger a massive witch-hunt or further erode confidence in government. This problem was particularly acute under De la Madrid because the anticorruption movement initiated by the government found much fertile ground among the public. To counteract the tendency of the anticorruption campaign to exaggerate the problem, De la Madrid stressed honesty in government and underscored the widespread corruption within society. Thus in 1983, the president suggested that "it is inadmissible that the sanctioning of high level public officials . . . detract from the high prestige of the great majority of workers in service to the state."[34]

The second danger of the anticorruption campaign stems from the question of how to deal with former presidents and their corruption. It is only natural for the heightened anticorruption sentiments mobilized during a campaign to prompt calls for the prosecution of the biggest fish of all; but many contend that such a move would have profound implications for the power and prestige of the office and the workings of the political system. Thus though certain patterns can be detected as to who are and who are not the victims of an anticorruption campaign, it is considered politically taboo to go after a former president (and interior secretary) because, as one observer notes, they "have something on everyone."[35] Still, both López Portillo and De la Madrid sustained strong public calls for the investigation of their respective predecessors.[36] Although an official denouncement was registered and a hot congressional debate ensued, the charges against López Portillo, decried by officials of the PRI as "counterrevolutionary" and a tactic by "traditional enemies of the PRI," were eventually dropped.[37] The refusal to pursue the López Portillo case eventually cost De la Madrid and his anticorruption campaign much credibility.

A final and most poignant characteristic of the anticorruption campaigns concerns their general failure to bring about fundamental change, despite the optimism and hope they inspire. The following assessment of Echeverría's anticorruption drive starkly contrasts with the widespread corruption that would mark the end of the president's term: "Echeverría . . . began to attack the laziness, incompetence and corruption of government bureaucrats in terms far more pointed than had been used by a Mexican official in two decades. He named names; . . . and he declared himself dedicated to altering the very concept of public office, which he asserted 'is regarded by many so-called public servants as booty.' "[38] Yet years later, a spokesman for the opposition National Action party (PAN) would charge that corruption under the Echeverría administration reached "scandalous proportions."[39] A similar situation of dashed hopes occurred under López Portillo.[40] Despite the optimistic evaluations of the president's programs during the initial years, the term ended in a free-for-all of corruption that many felt overshadowed that of previous administrations. The force and optimism attending De la Madrid's campaign also faded as the years wore on. Sol Sanders states that by the latter years "De la Madrid's 'Renovacion Moral' ha[d] become a farce, overwhelmed by the magnitude of its task and the refusal of the regime to make the sharp, political break with the past"; one U.S. State Department official asserted that "there has not really been the type of crackdown on corruption that most people think is needed."[41] The renewal of blatant electoral fraud in the latter half of his term, the assassination of journalists, including Manuel Buendía, reports produced early during the year of Hidalgo suggesting that the president had transferred between $10 and $20 million out of the country and that "others around the president have begun helping themselves to the public coffers,"[42] and a scandalous incident in 1988 in which the head of the judicial police for the state of Mexico was tortured and murdered by members of the Mexico City force were all part of the increased corruption. The scandal led not only to the indictment of seven high-level officers amid fears of the outbreak of civil war between the two neighboring police corps, but it also triggered public statements by the new chief of police about continuing abuses and corruption among the police.[43] Rooting out police corruption had been a major component of De la Madrid's program.

But as in previous anticorruption campaigns, the true legacy of the De la Madrid campaign was fashioned by his successor.

Within a broad strategy of "modernization," Salinas had within the first year produced a number of anticorruption victims and scandals, including the removal of Governors Xicoténcatl Leyva Montera of Baja California and Luis Martínez Villicana of Michoacán for suspected improprieties and of Eduardo Legorreta of the Operadora Bolsa for stock market and financial fraud; the military-led arrest of the powerful petroleum union leaders Joaquín Hernández Galícia (La Quina) and Salvador Barragán Camacho, four officials of BANRURAL, various police, including officials of the Mexico City Intelligence Directorate that led to the elimination of that body, and the former director of the Federal Security Directorate, José Antonio Zorrilla Perez, for the 1986 murder of journalist Manuel Buendía.[44] In accordance with the functions of the anticorruption campaign, these moves helped dissociate the new team from the previous one and bolster the president's popularity while discrediting his predecessor.

Thus in amazing contrast to the optimism that marked the dawn of Moral Renovation, Salinas's tough stand against corruption has helped paint the period of De la Madrid as *"el sexenio de la impunidad"* (impunity), marked by the protection of syndical *caciques*, speculators, *narcos*, police, and electoral fraud.[45] Governor Leyva, for instance, had been denounced in the legislature in 1984, and the former secretary of the treasury, Gustavo Petricioli Iturbide, has been accused of having known and protected the fraud in the financial sector with De la Madrid's knowledge.[46] The impression is widespread that De la Madrid was largely unconcerned about high- and mid-level police corruption and that eventually he came to believe that publicizing the problems of the system was counterproductive.[47]

The case of Zorrilla, in particular, raised staggering questions about the role of high-level officials, including the former president himself. As attention centered on the crime and possible cover-up, Margo Su of *La Jornada* stressed the need to know "who gave [Zorrilla] the order to execute the reporter who had no price;" Rafael Moya García of *El Universal* called for an explanation of the "zero efficiency in solving [the case] of the [former capital attorneys general] Victoria Adato and Sales Gasque";[48] and the editor of the *Mexico Journal* asked the ringing question, "How much did De la Madrid (and Bartlett Díaz [interior secretary] and so on) know, and when did he know it?"[49]

Reminiscent of similar circumstances at other times, the opposition's efforts to investigate top officials, including the former president, were again thwarted by the PRI majority. Senator Porfirio Muñoz Ledo of the center-left PRD (Party of the Democratic Revolution) demanded an investigation of De la Madrid for speculative activity prior to devaluations (including alleged deposits in foreign banks) and illegalities involving the privatization of public firms, an official exploration of the charges of corruption leveled against the president by Jack Anderson in 1984, and an investigation of the possible high-level cover-up of the Buendía assassination. Despite their desire for "the answers to come from the top officials in the last *sexenio*," proposals by opposition deputies to force the former president and former interior secretary to appear before the commission to explain their possible role in these crimes were overturned by the PRI majority.[50]

Nevertheless, true to form, Salinas's flamboyant actions contributed to the president's increasing popularity, convincing many of his resolve finally to deal with corruption. Independent polls in mid-1989, for instance, showed Salinas's rising support in Michoacán and Baja California, although this increased support was not shared by the PRI, and a nationwide poll in late 1989 showed that 79 percent of respondents approved of his actions.[51] The move against tax evaders even gained the praise of some on the left.[52] But others feel that the methods remain the same. They note that Salinas replaced Hernández Galícia and his group with a similar group led by Sebastian Guzmán Cabrera and that to limit the list of the guilty in the stock market scandal to Legorreta and four others was hardly attacking the corruption there.[53]

Despite the similarities in these campaigns, there were major differences among them, particularly those of López Portillo and De la Madrid, in intensity, priority, and duration: De la Madrid's campaign was greater on all three counts than the crusade carried out under López Portillo. The administrative reforms of López Portillo were only indirectly related to curbing corruption, whereas De la Madrid's reforms were targeted directly at corruption; Moral Renovation enjoyed high presidential priority during De la Madrid's term, but López Portillo's program was of lesser overall importance; and although the intensity of both campaigns declined markedly as their terms wore on, De la Madrid's campaign, though beleaguered, remained in the public light into the middle and later years of his term. Like López Portillo's, Salinas's campaign is encapsuled within a broader program of political and economic change, although with greater rhetorical emphasis on free elections.

To a large extent, these differences reflect major changes in popular feelings of diffuse system legitimacy during the two periods and thus on the role of the anticorruption device to mobilize popular support. The economic situation of the country was acutely grim throughout De la Madrid's term but not under López Portillo. The corruption theme was not only an important issue around which to mobilize the public, but it also helped take attention away from the nation's economic problems.

The failures of the reforms to do more than temporarily curb corruption demonstrate its intractable nature. Part of the reason the campaigns failed was that they did not fundamentally alter the nature of the state-society balance. Yet looking beyond these cyclical shifts, certain secular trends accentuated by the economic and political changes wrought by the 1980s do seem to indicate alterations in the state-society balance that affect the underlying causes of corruption.

6 Corruption and Public Opinion

Any discussion of political corruption raises important questions about popular attitudes and perceptions. It is therefore crucial to ask how the Mexican people actually feel about corruption. Addressing this question provides an additional means of testing some conclusions and propositions made earlier. This chapter, based on a 1986 survey, presents data that help gauge the extent of corruption in Mexico, detect some of the more predominant patterns of corruption, relate broad perceptions of Mexican politics to those on corruption, profile the impact of one anticorruption campaign, and underscore the forces of change underlying the 1980s. The data also offer an initial means of exploring possible determinants shaping these views.[1]

The survey involved over seven hundred interviews conducted in the cities of Huejotzingo, Puebla, and Mexico City in March 1986. The sampling design entailed a stratified group of twenty-seven public sites (parks, shopping centers, markets, subway stations, and *centros*) in the three locations: a rural village (Huejotzingo), a large provincial city (Puebla), and the capital city (Mexico City). The survey sites were selected to guarantee a suitable mixture of upper-, middle-, and lower-class respondents; the respondents at each site were chosen simply on the basis of convenience.[2]

It is important to emphasize that since the polling was not based on a totally random sample, the results can only be considered suggestive and not representative of the population as a whole. In addition, the poll measured opinion (as do all surveys) only at a single time; therefore the prevailing political climate, at the height of De la Madrid's anticorruption campaign and a severe economic crisis, should be borne in mind when interpreting the results. Still, both the large number of respondents and the diversity of their class status enhance the reliability of the data.

The survey contained three essential parts. The first focused on the perceived frequency of corruption in Mexico, generally as well as specifically. Respondents were asked about the perceived need to pay the *mordida*, about the accuracy of reports of corruption in Mexico, and about the relative frequency of certain corrupt acts. The second part examined popular evaluations of corruption as a national problem and as a cause of the nation's economic crisis. Respondents were asked to rank order corruption together with other national problems. The last portion pursued evaluations of the reforms of De la Madrid's anticorruption campaign. The questions centered on the reform's effectiveness in increasing honesty in government and the adequacy of De la Madrid's prosecution of corrupt officials.

Attitudes toward Corruption

The first set of questions sought to explore perceptions of the frequency of corruption in Mexico. The data clearly confirm that corruption is perceived to be widespread and is generally expected by the population. Slightly more than 78 percent of respondents felt that it was normally necessary to pay a bribe to resolve a matter with the government; less than 20 percent said bribes were needed only occasionally. In addition, a majority (54 percent) felt that the reports of corruption in Mexico did not accurately depict the extent of the practice, and only 19 percent thought the reports were exaggerated. The data show the types of corruption thought to occur most frequently. As shown in Table 6.1, petty police bribery and extortion, followed by peculation and bureaucratic bribery and extortion were deemed the most widespread; the least common acts among those listed included the improper release of criminals and ghost workers.

Although corruption was clearly perceived to be ubiquitous, its relative importance as an urgent national problem or cause of the economic crisis, the second component in the study, was not exceedingly high. Ranked among such isues as the Central American conflict, inflation, relations with the United States, the debt, agricultural production, and unemployment, corruption fell in the middle range, usually behind the pressing economic problems. Nor was corruption considered a major cause of the nation's economic crisis when compared to low petroleum prices, the devaluation of the peso, relations with the United States, the debt, low levels of productivity, and labor demands, again ranking in the middle range. Nonetheless, more than a quarter of the respondents (28 percent), identified corruption as Mexico's most urgent national problem and slightly more than 20 percent cited corruption as the principal determinant of the economic downturn.

Finally, the survey explored popular assessments of De la Madrid's campaign of Moral Renovation. The data show that a majority felt the reforms had increased honesty in government at least some (54.3 percent). Yet a much larger majority indicated that the extent of prosecution of corrupt officials was inadequate. The fact that over 80 percent of the respondents shared the view that the government was not adequately investigating and prosecuting public officials for corruption clearly suggests the widespread belief that government officials enjoy impunity for their actions.

Table 6.1. Frequency Rankings of Corrupt Acts

Type of Corrupt Activity	Percent Ranking Highest/Lowest	Mean Ranking
A person pays a bribe to police to avoid a traffic citation (n = 664)	42.5/6.0	2.7
A government official takes money from the government (n = 624)	23.6/7.9	3.4
A person pays a bribe to speed up a bureaucratic matter (n = 619)	13.9/6.6	3.6
A government official provides a government job to a family member (n = 617)	6.0/13.3	4.2
A government official makes a government decision that benefits his own private business (conflict of interest) (n = 619)	8.1/15.2	4.3
A criminal buys his freedom (n = 622)	5.9/20.6	4.6
A worker arrives at a job only to be paid (ghost worker) (n = 664)	8.9/35.9	5.0

The Influence of Trust, Socioeconomic Status, and Party Identification

Before examining the impact of certain variables on these opinions, it is first important to explore the relationships among the views themselves. Do they tap a common underlying opinion on corruption, or do they indicate independent dimensions of public opinion? Statistical analysis showed the two rankings of corruption (as a national problem and a cause of the economic crisis) to be closely linked (R = .48 at .10 of significance or less), as were the two evaluations of the reforms (gamma = .64, tau-b .30); however, assessments of the frequency of corruption showed no or a very weak correlation to either the rankings or reform evaluations.[3] This suggests that perceptions of the frequency of corruption have virtually no impact on one's evaluation of the problem or efforts to resolve it.

The data show a weak yet significant correlation between certain attitudes expressed and trust in government. Generally, respondents exhibiting less trust in the government were more likely to consider corruption more common, a more serious national problem, and a cause of the economic crisis and more likely to issue harsh appraisals of the anticorruption campaign than those demonstrating higher levels of trust in the government. Table 6.2 shows that 20 percent of those expressing high trust in government ranked the need to bribe as low compared to 5.7 percent of those with low levels of trust. Table 6.3 reveals that 32 percent of the respondents with high trust in government offered a negative evaluation of the Moral Renovation campaign compared to 62 percent of those expressing low levels of trust.

The data also show a weak yet significant tendency for older, male respondents and those from Mexico City to rank corruption higher as a national problem than younger, female respondents from the other two cities in the sample. With the

Table 6.2. Perceived Need to Bribe by Trust in Government (in percent)

Need to Bribe	Level of Trust		
	High	Medium	Low
High	22.5	35.0	55.3
Medium-high	40.0	43.3	32.4
Medium-low	17.5	18.1	6.5
Low	20.0	3.7	5.7
gamma = −.36		tau-c = −.21	

exception of respondents from Mexico City who tended to view corruption as more common than respondents from the other two locations, these factors had no effect on opinions of frequency or evaluations of the reforms. For example, though only 16 percent of the respondents from Mexico City felt that reports of corruption were exaggerated, 23 percent in the other two locations expressed this view.

Socioeconomic factors were considered to explore the impact of income and education on opinions on corruption. In general, the data show a tendency for those with higher so-

Table 6.3. Evaluation of Anticorruption Reforms by Trust in Government (in percent)

Evaluation	Level of Trust		
	High	Medium	Low
Positive	22.6	9.1	5.3
Mediocre	45.2	55.7	32.1
Negative	32.1	35.1	62.2
gamma = .42		tau-b = .26	

Table 6.4. Evaluation of Anticorruption Reforms by
Education (in percent)

| | Education | | | |
Evaluation	High	High-Middle	Low-Middle	Low
Positive	6.4	5.9	9.5	16.8
Mediocre	41.2	46.4	52.1	45.0
Negative	51.9	47.7	38.5	38.2
	gamma = −.19		tau-c = −.11	

cioeconomic status to view corruption as a more significant
national problem and more frequent and tended to express a
slightly more negative appraisal of the reforms than respondents from lower socioeconomic categories. For example, 38
percent of the high-income group ranked corruption as the nation's most pressing issue compared to 31 percent of the upper-
middle group, 29 percent of the lower-middle, and 24 percent of
the low-income group. Similarly, 34 percent viewed corruption
as the principal cause of the economic crisis compared to 25
percent of the upper-middle group, 20 percent of the lower-middle group, and 10 percent of the low-income group. Table 6.4
shows that 6 percent of college-educated respondents gave a
positive evaluation of the anticorruption reforms and 52 percent a negative assessment compared to 17 percent and 38 percent respectively for those with only an elementary school
education. Similarly, as shown in Table 6.5, only 12 percent of
the highest-educated group considered the reports of corruption to be exaggerated compared to 33 percent among the
lowest-educated group. In fact, a majority of respondents with
low levels of education either considered the reports of corruption accurate or exaggerated.

Finally, focus on political involvement explored the impact
of party identification, voting, and interest in politics on at-

Table 6.5. Evaluation of Reports of Corruption by Education (in percent)

Reports	Education			
	High	High-Middle	Low-Middle	Low
Exaggerated	12.1	18.2	20.0	32.8
Accurate	22.9	27.9	36.4	26.0
Understated	64.9	53.9	43.6	41.2
	gamma = −.27		tau-c = −.18	

titudes toward corruption. As would be expected, those identifying with the PRI were slightly more likely to rank corruption lower as a national problem, interpret reports of corruption as exaggerated, and harbor more positive evaluations of the reforms than those identifying with opposition parties. Generally, the views of nonpartisans fell somewhere in between. For example, 24 percent of PRI identifiers gauged corruption as the nation's most pressing issue compared to 34 percent among those identifying with the opposition and 28 percent of nonpartisans. As Table 6.6 shows, 26 percent of PRI identifiers compared to 11 percent of those identifying with the opposition and 17 percent of nonpartisans expressed the view that the reports of corruption in Mexico were exaggerated. Table 6.7 similarly shows that among PRI identifiers, 32 percent held a negative view of the reforms compared to 56 percent of respondents identifying with the opposition and 49 percent of nonpartisans.

Voting frequency of the respondents revealed no significant effect on any of the opinions toward corruption, though a respondent's expressed level of interest in politics appeared to be slightly related to evaluations of corruption as a national problem. Among those indicating a high level of interest in politics, for instance, 39 percent viewed corruption as the nation's most

Table 6.6. Evaluation of Reports of Corruption by Party
Identification (in percent)

Reports	Party Identification		
	PRI and affiliates	Nonpartisan	Opposition
Exaggerated	26.2	17.4	11.5
Accurate	29.9	30.3	19.5
Understated	43.9	52.3	69.0
	gamma = .10	tau-b = .06	

urgent problem compared to 20 percent and 25 percent at the midrange and low levels of interest.

Attempting to control for the effects of third variables when using ordinal measures is statistically difficult because the number of cases in each cell is usually too small. But because trust in government was affected by location, party identification, and interest in politics, the impact of these variables on attitudes toward corruption was tested while controlling for trust. Although inconclusive, the data suggest that party identification played a moderate role on ranking, evaluations of re-

Table 6.7. Evaluation of Anticorruption Reforms by
Party Identification (in percent)

Evaluation	Party Identification		
	PRI and affiliates	Nonpartisan	Opposition
Positive	15.0	6.5	7.0
Mediocre	53.2	43.8	36.8
Negative	31.8	49.5	56.1
	gamma = .24	tau-b = .15	

form, and reports at all levels of trust, while the relationship between location (Mexico City) and interest in politics on corruption-related views appeared to be largely spurious. This means that the tendency for those with high levels of interest to hold less critical views of corruption reflected this group's greater trust in government, and the tendency for respondents from Mexico City to harbor harsher views on corruption basically reflected their tendency to express lower levels of trust in government.

Analysis and Discussion of the Results

The data suggest a number of tentative conclusions. First, the descriptive data clearly indicate that the public perceives corruption to be widespread. Most respondents felt that politicians exploit public office with impunity, that the police system is highly corrupt, and that the payment of the *mordida* is a routine institutional feature in dealing with the government.

Second, the data offer some support for the hypothesis that corruption has contributed to widespread distrust of the government. The relationship between trust in government and views on corruption, however, is not clear-cut. It seems likely that a reciprocal linkage exists rather than a unidirectional one, with specific opinions on corruption forging a part of the basic attitudes on trust (inductive) and broad feelings of trust in government providing the initial cues and predispositions to evaluate corruption and anticorruption reforms (deductive). Hence though corruption is not entirely responsible for popular distrust of the government, it certainly adds to it, as the culture of corruption thesis suggests.

Third, although it is impossible to gauge the effectiveness of anticorruption campaigns generally based on the views expressed here, the data do show that the Moral Renovation campaign of De la Madrid was somewhat successful during its initial period in increasing the perceived level of honesty in government. This is particularly noteworthy despite the perceived frequency of corruption and the general view that the prosecution of officials from the previous administration was grossly inadequate. When combined with the results from more recent polls showing high approval ratings for Salinas in his first year in office,[4] it does appear that anticorruption measures are easy means of bolstering political support.

A related question is whether the distrust bred by widespread corruption actually leads to a decline of legitimacy or antisystem behavior, prompting mobilizations and instability. Earlier it was argued that the anticorruption device has prevented such a potentially destabilizing outcome historically. Unfortunately, no direct measure of support for the system was employed in the poll. Using identification with the PRI as an indicator of such support,[5] however, indicates that despite the tendency for corruption to translate into low levels of trust in the government, trust treated as the independent variable was unrelated to identification with the PRI. As shown in Table 6.8, the same percentage of respondents with low and high levels of trust identified with the official party, although when viewed from the opposite perspective, those in the party exhibited a weak tendency toward more trust in the government compared to members of the opposition. In other words, low levels of trust in government or negative evaluations of government performance apparently have not translated into a mass exodus away from the official "system" party and toward the opposition. This suggests that although corruption may promote feelings of distrust and cynicism, it does not exhibit a strong tendency to produce behavior against the system or the mobilization of the opposition, as suggested earlier.

Yet it does appear that diffuse support may be lower today than in the past: the numbers identifying with the PRI were much lower than those recorded by a survey done in 1978–79.[6] Indeed, the extremely low levels of trust and high expectation

Table 6.8. Party Identification by Trust in Government (in percent)

Party Identification	Trust in Government		
	Low	Medium	High
PRI and affiliates	26	32	26
Nonpartisan	53	55	53
Opposition	21	13	21

of corruption registered here suggest that corruption may have reached such levels that it is compromising the system's capacity to maintain popular support. This cannot be confirmed without longitudinal data. Still, analyses of the impact of the economic crisis on corruption in the next chapter identify the heightened level of anticorruption protest during this period.

Also significant is that corruption is interpreted as more of problem by those identifying with the opposition than by non-partisans or PRI identifiers. This suggests that either the opposition has successfully mobilized an anticorruption political sentiment or that those feeling strongly about the problem of corruption have become mobilized into political action.

Fourth, the data suggest that those more likely to have contacts with government tend to harbor more cynical views toward corruption. This view would seem to account for the fact that younger people, females, and those not living in the center of political activity (Mexico City) expressed different opinions than their older, male, Mexico City counterparts. Males, for instance, are far more likely to encounter the police in a given day than females.

In addition, the data reveal that those from higher socioeconomic backgrounds tend to be more critical of corruption than those from lower socioeconomic groups. This may reflect a confluence of factors, including the influence of education in instilling values antithetical to corruption or a lesser concern about materialistic matters and greater interest in ethical, postmaterialist problems among such sectors. Clearly, those of lower socioeconomic standing tend to view economic problems as relatively more urgent. This pattern also suggests that as Mexico develops, greater opposition to corruption may materialize, as predicted by much of the modernization literature.

Finally, the perceived need to bribe was largely unrelated to any of the other measures except for a very weak correlation with trust in government. This suggests that although socioeconomic status or party identification may affect evaluations of corruption and anticorruption reforms (good-bad), they do not seem overly to determine perceptions of the extent of corruption in the political system. This indicates an important distinction between absolute levels of corruption, on one hand, and corruption in relation to other problems, perceived reports of corruption, or the past (effect of reforms), on the other.

The results provide an empirical basis for profiling popular views on corruption in Mexico at a particular time and are therefore clearly limited. It is virtually impossible to assess whether such views resemble attitudes of a previous period or whether they signify a significant change regarding the extent, role, or reaction to political corruption. Indeed, the changing economic and political climate that prevailed during the period when the poll was taken raises questions about the dynamics of the corruption equation. Despite the conventional role of corruption in Mexico, is it possible that historic forces have altered that role or the state-society balance that forges corruption? To address this question, attention now turns to the tumultuous decade of the 1980s, which, among other things, seemed to elevate the issue of corruption in Mexico to new heights.

7 The "Crisis of Corruption" in the 1980s

Heretofore, analysis of the causes and consequences of corruption in Mexico has assumed a basically historical posture, premised on explaining how widespread corruption flowed from and contributed to a remarkably stable regime. But since 1982, Mexico and the Mexican political system have undergone significant changes: the once booming economy has plummeted and the once stable political machine has deteriorated. Increasingly, observers ponder Mexico's political future and the very survivability of Latin America's oldest political regime: "whether the system has enough flexibility and resiliency to respond to the new circumstances brought on by modernizing changes and pressures or whether it will become steadily more discredited, inefficient, and, finally, prone to collapse or even overthrow."[1]

In many ways, political corruption stands at the center of the controversy; it shapes alternatives and, many feel, is a major catalyst of the nation's recent ills. This chapter explores three sets of factors crucial in understanding the interrelationships between the ongoing crises and changes of the 1980s and political corruption, or what is referred to here as the "crisis of corruption."

The first thesis associates the heightened attention and

115

opposition to corruption characterizing the period with the high-profile anticorruption campaign of De la Madrid and the critical economic decline. It draws from earlier discussions of the anticorruption campaigns and the conditions for the stabilizing consequences of corruption. The second thesis links the increased awareness of and concern over corruption to changes in the patterns of corruption that occurred during the late 1970s and early 1980s. This includes what many interpret as accelerating corruption reflecting an abrupt and pronounced shift in the state-society balance during the prosperous oil boom years (1978–81), qualitative changes related to the centralization of corruption at higher levels, and the rise of perhaps destabilizing drug-related corruption.

Finally, the third thesis centers on the impact of fundamental changes in the state-society balance associated with the crisis and changes designed to adapt to it on corruption. It holds that the weakening of the state combined with burgeoning mobilizations and autonomy of social organizations and the increasing politicization of elections and resounding challenges to the legitimacy of the PRI have forced corruption into the limelight, perhaps altering its effects and turning this once stabilizing ingredient of the system into a liability. Such forces alter the sociopolitical equation and may therefore impinge on the incidence of corruption. Politically, though, corruption remains critical in assisting the PRI in staving off the strong challenges and threats to its hegemony.

The Crises of the 1980s

In the decade of the 1980s Mexico endured a multifaceted array of deeply rooted and interwoven political and economic setbacks.[2] Economically, the country confronted a massive foreign debt (U.S. $107 billion by 1987) and internal debts, high interest rates, low world petroleum prices (the nation's major export), a stagnant world economy, and massive capital flight. National income fell in 1982, 1983, and 1986, and slow growth in the other years resulted in lower per capita income in 1988 than a decade earlier. The value of the peso plummeted from 25 to the dollar at the beginning of the decade to approximately 2,650 at the end; inflation gained momentum during the mid-decade years, reaching 159 percent before a solidarity pact between business, government, and labor elaborated in December 1987 slowed its pace. By 1987 unemployment stood at 17.6 percent, and real minimum wages had fallen by 41.9 percent since 1982.[3]

With poverty compounding poverty, it is clear that the persistent economic troubles wore on the people's hope and optimism for a better future and their confidence in the government. In a *New York Times* poll in 1986, for example, 61 percent of the respondents said the economic situation would get worse in the following year, and 54 percent believed that Mexico would never emerge from its economic crisis. Politically, the discontent took on an electoral expression, altering the nature of Mexican elections and challenging the PRI's hegemony.

Politics historically rarely entered into the electoral arena; accommodations among elite sectors were forged through other, less public channels and solidified in part with corruption. Even electoral fraud helped to foreclose a highly mobilizational and potentially destabilizing channel and redirect political demand making into its proper avenues. But as the administrative/accommodative channels proved incapable of handling the increasingly contradictory demands, conflict and discontent spilled over into the electoral arena, often encouraged by the government. The decade thus saw the political focal point and epicenter shift to elections, attracting both national and international attention.

In this process, the PRI faced formidable challenges. From 1983 to 1985, the rightist PAN recorded numerous electoral victories in such key municipalities as Chihuahua and Ciudad Juárez and orchestrated strong protests and civil disturbances in response to blatant electoral fraud in other areas such as Durango, Oaxaca, and Zacatecas. Then in 1987, the PRI suffered a major internal division when the left-nationalist wing led by former Michoacán Governor Cuauhtémoc Cárdenas Solórzano and former PRI director and ambassador to the United States Porfirio Muñoz Ledo broke from the party to forge a formidable alliance of the center-left that, together with other opposition parties, rapidly mobilized to challenge the government's legitimacy. In the national elections a year later, the government conceded the loss of four Senate seats to the Cárdenas-led front, witnessed its huge majority in the legislature shrink to a handful, and was forced to resort to high-level fraud to maintain control of the presidency. The deplorable handling of the national vote precludes certainty about the result, yet one national survey found that a mere 24 percent of the population actually believed that Salinas was the true victor.[4] Since the 1988 elections, the opposition, pinching from both the right and left, has continued to pressure the PRI electorally, yielding victories in some areas (PAN's victory in the gubernatorial election in Baja being the most notable) and mobilizing against electoral fraud in others.

An accompanying feature of these electoral changes has been the rise of more autonomous social organizations. These include popular organizations, independent unions, and political organizations, as well as growing press and public criticism of the system and even the president (long considered taboo). Also accompanying these political changes is the conspicuous crisis of corruption.

The crisis of corruption nurtures and is nurtured by the nation's ominous political difficulties. Subsumed within the political crisis, the crisis of corruption involves heightened levels of public attention and opposition to political corruption; the rise of popular organizations and mobilizations protesting and exposing corrupt officials, including electoral fraud; and the proliferation of the view that though perhaps once helping to stabilize the system, corruption has begun to undermine the regime's stability. As one student describes it, "Never in its history has the Mexican public been so conscious of the problem of official corruption at all levels."[6]

The rise of protests, strikes, and demonstrations focusing directly or indirectly on the theme of corruption provides one indication of this crisis of corruption marking the decade. A strike by truckers in the states of Durango, Sinaloa, and Sonora as well as protests led by unions in Naucalpan in the state of Mexico in 1983, for example, centered on the extortionist practices of the police.[7] Even a prison riot at the Eastern Penitentiary in Mexico City in December 1985 featured demands for the end to corrupt payments for clothes, food, and family visits.[8] Increasingly, it seemed that the decade transformed demands for nominal changes in public policy into demands for the proper implementation of already existing policies.[9]

Besides spawning greater protests, the crisis of corruption also finds many who perhaps once viewed corruption as contributing to the stability of the regime now issuing much harsher appraisals. The spread and acceptance of such views clearly alter the perceived need to deal with corruption as a political problem. For example, although corruption had only a minimal impact on the economic crisis, it has received much of the blame for the nation's economic ills. Many public leaders say that corruption has undermined the economy. The PAN presidential candidate in 1982, for instance, stated unequivocally that "corruption is the principal cause of the [economic] crisis," and the bishop of Tuxtla Gutiérrez, Chiapas, averred that corruption did more harm to the economy than the major devaluation of the period.[10]

Some, however, go even further in decrying corruption as the root of the country's ailments. In 1982, for example, the former president of the Supreme Court warned that corruption put the country at risk of falling to dictatorship.[11] John Gavin, the former U.S. ambassador to Mexico, posited that corruption yields nothing but ill: "All of the many problems of Mexico, from the economy, to drugs, to mass migration, to the lack of democracy, are the results of a system that is corrupt."[12]

Perhaps the clearest indication of change in the 1980s with regard to corruption is the emergence of specifically anticorruption organizations. La Liga Mexicana Anti-Corrupto (Mexican Anti-Corruption League), for example, founded in 1981 for the purpose of denouncing corruption and pressuring the government for prosecutions of corrupt officials, is composed of some twenty-six civic organizations and enjoys strong ties to the rightist opposition party, the Social Democratic party (PSD). La Fundación contra la Corrupción (Foundation against Corruption)[13] and El Movimiento Popular Anti-Corrupción (MPA) (Popular Anti-Corruption Movement) both began their crusades against corruption in 1983. The MPA was particularly active in denouncing fraud in Ciudad Victoria and later in the Banco Confía.[14] In Hermosillo, Sonora, a group called Consciencia Ciudana (Citizen's Conscience) sponsored a public program entitled "no al soborno" ("no to bribery") and has exposed fraud in local PEMEX service stations. Although made up basically of PAN partisans, the group enjoys widespread support throughout the state.[15]

In interpreting the crises, two preliminary points are warranted. Often a dialectical relationship exists between the various crises such that a policy response designed to temper one may exacerbate the other. Reducing the federal deficit or cutting official union privileges to confront economic problems, for example, may undermine the regime's political capacity to co-opt its opponents; yet refusing to pursue such changes for political reasons equally encumbers the economic problems. Contradictions among the crises may result in political dilemmas, contrasting trends, and paradoxical behavior that affect the nature and incidence of political corruption. Moreover, an analytical distinction should be drawn between the effects of a crisis per se and the effects of the policies fashioned to manage the crisis. Thus real, potential, or perceived changes in political corruption may stem from either the political and economic crises themselves or the policy changes that seek to resolve them (or some combination of the two).

Scarce Resources and the Anticorruption Campaign

The first set of factors contributing to the crisis of corruption centers on the economic crisis and the anticorruption campaign. The economic crisis reduced the quantity of resources available to the regime, thereby altering the functioning of corruption in the system. Among the elite, the scarcity of resources disrupted a previously stable and prosperous system by introducing greater competition, turning a positive-sum game into a zero-sum match. This greatly complicates the accommodative game and erodes the regime's ability to "buy" support at a time when it is most desperately needed. Yet despite the increased competition, the economic crisis failed to subdue the thirsts of those who had patiently awaited their opportunity to partake of the system's spoils. In fact, by shaking the elite's trust in the system's ability to continue to reward pragmatism and political obedience and by prompting images of the system's collapse, the economic decline may have yielded a "get what you can" mentality.

For the general public, the economic crisis equally transformed corruption. First, it lowered the threshold of what long constituted acceptable or permissible levels of corruption. The public came to feel, for instance, that the brunt of austerity programs and cutbacks fashioned in response to the economic crisis should be borne by the political elite before they themselves are called upon to make any sacrifices.[16] The ill-gotten gains of the nation's political leaders that could once be overlooked became a source of intense frustration and protest.

Second, the economic decline accentuated and exposed the mismanagement, inefficiencies, and general inability of the government to pursue its nominal goals. As the problems of the masses and particularly the middle class become more urgent and transparent and the demands more vocal, the ability of corruption to smooth the operation of the system and oil the cracks declined. Samuel P. Huntington posits that corruption, once a substitute for reform, came to be seen as insufficient to respond to the major systemic contradictions being exposed.[17]

In addition to and closely linked to the impact of the economic crisis, the crisis of corruption also reflects the high-profile anticorruption campaign of De la Madrid. In itself a political response to the economic crisis, the anticorruption drive helped shape the prevailing view that corruption contributed to the economic dilemma and had become a political liability. Indeed, many of the outcries and mobilizations against corruption of the 1980s were staged or triggered by the government in a well-orchestrated effort to use corruption symbolically to divert attention away from the economic difficulties and rejuvenate popular faith in the government: the typical anticorruption tactic. Corruption may be the only issue on which the government and the public can agree, particularly during dire economic times. A concerted effort to fight it thus helps mobilize support when it is most needed.

Anticorruption campaigns have long been a common feature of Mexican politics, yet the force of the anticorruption wave of the 1980s, although eventually discredited, clearly surpassed previous efforts. It was an ordinary political response to an extraordinary situation. But though the campaign was orchestrated to mobilize the public, control excessive graft, and deflect attention from other problems, indications are that it took root with the public, resulting in often uncontrolled pro-

tests against corruption. Although the force of the official campaign stagnated toward the latter part of De la Madrid's term,
popular anticorruption sentiments waxed.

It is virtually impossible to determine the exact extent to
which the anticorruption campaign contributed to the crisis of
corruption and hence whether corruption has actually become
destabilizing. Although it has clearly undermined political authority and trust in public officials, its importance does not
approach that of the economic crisis. If increased protests and
opposition to corruption created in large part by the anticorruption campaign helped divert attention away from the
nation's crucial economic or political problems, then it is possible that corruption may actually have enhanced overall stability, as it has historically. But to the extent that the
heightened awareness reflects changes in the conditions necessary for corruption to contribute to political stability or shake
government control, corruption may have become seriously destabilizing and far more costly than in the past.

Moreover, to the degree that the crisis of corruption reflects
the problem of economic scarcity and the anticorruption campaign, little has really changed. Indeed, once the situation of
resource scarcity abates, the corruption issue could fade and
the system could continue without significant alteration with
the relationship between corruption and stability restored. A
comparable situation prevailed in 1977. Mexico confronted
both a harsh economic crisis and a highly praised anticorruption campaign, both of which faded with the onset of the oil
boom in 1978. The economy rapidly turned around, corruption
increased, and stability was restored.

Changes in Corruption

A second explanation for the crisis of corruption hinges on
apparent changes in Mexican corruption during the decade.

Both quantitative and qualitative changes may have transformed a previously controlled and stabilizing component of the system into a costly political burden.

The perception is widespread that the level of corruption in the system increased enormously since the mid-1970s and, as a result, overstepped the bounds of contributing to the system's stability. This conclusion flows essentially from the reported high levels of corruption marking the final years of the López Portillo administration. A former adviser to De la Madrid, Samuel I. del Villar, underscores not only this change but also its pernicious effect: "What worries me is the velocity that corruption is accelerating through the government. It's the most serious threat to national security we face. If the government doesn't do something about it, it will destroy our country."[18] Riding makes a similar argument, suggesting that "a system that had never worked smoothly without corruption was no longer working smoothly because of excessive corruption."[19]

Although measuring the amount of corruption over time is difficult, most agree that corruption attained new heights and much greater exposure than ever before under the López Portillo administration, in part because of the abrupt and marked shift in the state-society balance accompanying the economic boom of the 1978–81 period. Government revenues from petroleum shot up at phenomenal rates, and the government expanded its programs proportionally, but internal and external checks lagged behind.[20] The result was increased public booty and fewer relative controls. The crisis of corruption may therefore represent in part an aftershock, an attempt by society to reassert some control over the state and the proclivities of state personnel.

But in addition to the rapid increase in the state's control of mobility opportunities during the 1978–81 period, three qualitative changes in corruption were apparent during this period that many feel strained the capacity of the system to maintain corruption within acceptable (stabilizing) limits. The first corresponded to the increases in oil revenues during the early part of the decade. Some feel that the heightened corruption associated with petroleum profits was not simply a quantitative increase but was more dangerous and destabilizing than the corruption of the past. Noting the higher stakes and payoffs and the monopolistic control over opportunities for corruption, Michael Johnston concludes that "the growth of oil revenues . . . placed extraordinary resources in many hands, transforming formerly integrative forms of corruption into disintegrative crisis of corruption."[21]

A second qualitative change consists of a shift in the bureaucratic locus of corruption. A strong perception prevails that corruption centered increasingly in the upper levels of the government rather than the lower levels as in the past: "Since the 1970s . . . the fruits of corruption began to move upward rather than downward. With top officials taking more for themselves and their bosses and sharing less with their political supporters, not only were larger illicit fortunes accumulated but this new wealth was also concentrated in fewer hands. Corruption was therefore working less as a system than as a racket and many of the traditional beneficiaries began to object."[22]

One possible reason for the upward shift of corruption may have been the often-noted decline of the traditional politicians and the ascendancy of the technocrats. Beginning with the López Portillo government, higher-level officials increasingly lacked experience in elected or political posts, coming instead from more technical bureaucracies. But why would the rise of the technocrats forge a new pattern of corruption? One possible reason is that the traditional *políticos* are tied to major constituent groups, such as labor or peasants, and therefore recognized certain limits on the amount of corruption they could engage in. Higher-level technocrats, however, are under no such constraints and therefore could potentially exploit their offices on a much grander scale. The plundering of the public coffers under López Portillo provides some support for this view.

But though the shift to technocratic leadership since the mid-1970s has clearly been accompanied by widespread corruption, it is not clear whether the two are causally related. Despite their perhaps more technocratic background and training, many of those involved in acquiring illicit political fortunes in the 1980s occupied clearly political posts such as governors, police chiefs, presidents, and union officials. In addition, data presented earlier suggest that at least at the lower levels, officials in technocratic areas are far more professional and less often associated with corruption than their counterparts occupying more political posts. Corruption in such political areas as the police, agrarian reform, unions, and petroleum, for instance, was particularly well represented in the data.

A third qualitative change in the decade was the proliferation of drug-related corruption, which, according to both Mexican and U.S. officials, has grown remarkably since the early 1980s.[23] The tremendous jump in cocaine seizures from thirteen pounds in 1982 to three tons in 1985 and five tons in the first seven months of 1986 provides one indication of the cocaine boom. Increasingly, politicians and particularly police have been attracted to this profitable enterprise.

The analysis of news articles tends to confirm this qualitative change. Although drug-related corruption has existed for years, no reports surfaced until 1980, when an official of the Sinaloa state judicial police was accused of bribery in the release of drug traffickers from police custody.[24] Since then, drug-related corruption has received more attention, and it is perhaps the most prevalent form of corruption covered by the press today. A host of scandals implicated federal judicial police, the military, and even higher-level officials such as state governors for cooperating with and even protecting drug traffickers.[25] The facts exposed in the Camarena and Buendía cases also revealed the extent of drug-related corruption.

Theoretically, it appears that this now prevalent form of corruption may be more destabilizing than traditional forms. Drug-related corruption falls into the category of bribery rather than extortion and, as a result, tends to divide the political elite and attract them to other avenues of social mobility rather than unite them behind the opportunities for mobility offered by the state.

Changes in the State-Society Balance

The third set of factors crucial in understanding the crisis of corruption relates to recent changes and trends in the state-society balance wrought by policies designed to confront the nation's economic and political difficulties. During the 1978–81 period the power of the state increased rapidly, but in subsequent years there was a gradual yet pronounced reversal of that process: the weakening of the state, the strengthening of social organizations, and an invigoration of the electoral arena. Certain trends suggest that these changes may be altering the role of corruption in the system and may eventually impinge on its incidence; yet other signs indicate continued reliance on corruption to stave off reform.

Basic changes in the state in response to the crisis include reductions in its size, the adoption of an economic model that requires the state to relinquish important controls over certain sectors of society, and the resurgence of elections and society. First, consistent with International Monetary Fund terms of conditionality for loans, the De la Madrid government endeavored to cut the size of the public sector. Among other measures, this included the firing of some fifty thousand bureaucrats in 1983, a program of administrative simplification initiated in 1984 that eliminated many government programs, the reduction and in some cases removal of price and production subsidies, and the gradual and timid process of privatization of public enterprises.[26] Central government expenditures fell from 27.1 percent of GDP in 1982 to 17.1 percent in 1988;[27] the public sector deficit dropped from a high of 11.9 percent of GDP in 1982 to 8.0 percent in 1985, with 30 percent devoted to interest payments alone.[28] Of the 1,214 state-owned firms in 1982, 756 were slated for disincorporation by mid-1988, although these accounted for only 3 percent of 1983 state-enterprise production, or 15 percent excluding PEMEX.[29] These policies have continued apace under Salinas, who, as secretary of planning and budgeting under De la Madrid, was in large part responsible for their design.

In addition to reductions in size, the government also embarked on a course of economic revitalization that envisages a less activist and interventionist state and a more open model of economic development. The cornerstone of this new model is Mexico's entry into the General Agreement on Tariffs and Trade (GATT) in 1986. This monumental decision means the abandonment of "a protectionist policy that had been a basic feature of the nation's internal development strategy since World War II."[30] Concomitant changes included reductions in the proportion of imports subject to licensing from 100 percent to 35 percent from 1983 to 1987 and the elimination of consumer and production subsidies and price controls.[31] The economic transformation, however, is slow and incremental, with much bureaucratic and political inertia to be overcome. The results should not be exaggerated.

Politically, the decline in state power has meant the invigoration of elections, a greater relative autonomy and political space for most social organizations, and changes in traditional government-labor and government-business relationships. The new role for elections finds not only the opposition adopting democracy as the central, overriding issue, challenging the PRI on a basic point along the system's legitimizing ideology, but "political democracy has become the linchpin of its [the government's] new legitimization efforts."[32] This has spawned, in turn, a strengthening of opposition parties and party politics and a more visible and influential role for the Congress. Combined with the political reforms under López Portillo and De la Madrid that allocated a greater number of seats in the National Chamber of Deputies to the opposition and created greater oversight powers for Congress,[33] these changes converted a once docile and tame institution into a formidable political arena.

In addition to the rise of opposition parties via the electoral track, private organizations have grown during the course of the decade and are "no longer totally dependent on the state for tutelary capitalist promotion."[34] This "creeping pluralism" or "relative weakening of the state" includes a basic change in interest group politics, with greater autonomy accruing to previously co-opted organizations, stretching what one analyst refers to as the "boundaries of permissibility."[35] The traditional modus operandi has changed even toward the media. As Daniel Levy suggests, "Overall . . . the media appear more free to criticize the government than they were fifteen, ten or even fewer years ago."[36]

These changes have also forged a new, far less cordial relationship between the government and official labor unions.[37] Hurt both by the economic emphasis on efficiency and the political emphasis on electoral support, the government has pursued policies clearly antithetical to the interests of entrenched labor. These policies include attacks on union privileges and union leaders, cutting back on such subsidies as sweetheart contracts,[38] rejecting the demands of Fidel Velázquez in negotiating the economic pact,[39] the use of disincorporation and bankruptcies to resolve labor disputes as in Fundidora, Aeroméxico, and Cananea, the nation's largest cooper-mining firm,[40] and the strikes against the petroleum union's powerful leaders Joaquín Hernández Galícia and Barragán Camacho. When combined with the deleterious loss of workers' purchasing power because of the economic crisis and resulting austerity measures, such moves erode mass support for the official unions, thereby enhancing the prospects for independent labor movements.[41]

The relationship between the government and the private sector also underwent significant change as a result of the new programs. Long politically subordinate, the business community began openly to challenge the state's legitimizing ideology during the 1980s, blaming Mexico's problems on the "failure [of the state] to recognize the 'natural right' of society to organize itself free from the control or tutelage of government." Taking advantage of new political openings, the business community sought organization to press its demands on the government more effectively. Many businessmen became politically more active, broke from the revolutionary circle, and began to support the opposition PAN openly.[42] A large part of this political activism was channeled into anticorruption organizations.

In sum, the Mexican state embarked on a series of reforms that envisage greater limitations on the power of the state, a greater reliance on the private sector, and greater political openness. Forces in society, in the meantime, pushed their own autonomy and demands with greater vigor than ever before. As an integral part of the political system, corruption is clearly affected by both the economic and political changes of the decade. To understand these implications it is important, however, to recall the somewhat paradoxical function of corruption in simultaneously integrating the elite while delegitimizing the system. Generally, both the economic and political changes make continued corruption a growing liability in the face of popular pressures for change, yet the need for elite integration becomes more critical.

The implications of the changes for corruption are many, although somewhat paradoxical. First, cutting back on the size of the state and its resource base greatly reduces the opportunities for corruption and decreases the state's capacity to control mobility opportunities. The Mexican bureaucracy has long depended on the expansion of its resource base to reward its supporters through opportunities for corruption, and cutting back on its growth seriously disrupts the continuity of this institutionalized game. The regime is increasingly unable to co-opt potential opponents because of the lack of resources or the pernicious effects such a lack would have on the private sector's ability to compete: a major component of the new economic model. Clearly, the capacity of the system to co-opt has declined.[43]

Second, by reducing its growth, the state diminished its attractiveness as a route of social mobility. If the state's potential for offering mobility once promoted corruption, then the reverse should eventually reduce it; if the opportunity for corruption fed stability, then its reduction can prove destabilizing. To an extent, this adds to the problems of legitimacy because the ambitions of those who might aspire to the once secure and fruitful public sector are neglected. For instance, one report suggested that De la Madrid's "key aides are said to believe that it is unfair for them to continue to try to reform a corrupt system just when it is their turn to exploit."[44]

Third, the strengthening autonomy of such sectors as the press or the scholarly community portends various consequences. More open debate, for instance, erodes the state's ability to propagate its own interpretation of events, thus creating a greater check on government power. By fostering greater professionalism among the press, this may also curtail the long tradition of press corruption. The local press in Hermosillo, Sonora, for example, which has strongly and routinely attacked corruption, began running a column in the mid-1980s entitled "Se di jo . . . y no se hizo" (Said . . . but not done). Such a role for the press was unheard-of in years past.

Fourth, the expanded visibility and role of the opposition, particularly in Congress, strengthened congressional oversight powers to check corruption. In 1980, when Congress denounced fraud in public works, triggering prosecutions, it was reportedly the first time the Chamber of Deputies had moved against corruption.[45] Since then, Congress (particularly the opposition) has played a far more active role in investigating and exposing political corruption. Opposition parties, for example, orchestrated the moves against López Portillo and Díaz Serrano and called for investigations of De la Madrid and Petricioli. In fact, it was the PSD that brought suit against López Portillo and twelve former officials for peculation of funds, the PAN that pressured the Justice Department for copies of López Portillo's statement of assets, and the Mexican Workers party (PMT) that registered the official denouncement against Díaz Serrano for fraud and later threatened to mobilize the population if the Justice Department did not pursue the case.[46] In October 1985, Congress investigated alleged "variations" in the budget of the Mexico City government, subpoenaing and questioning officials at great length.[47] Such a role is sure to continue as the opposition uses Congress as its major forum to express discontent.

Fifth, changes in the government-union relationship also greatly affect the nature of corruption in the system. Rooting out the perquisites of union officialdom for economic and political reasons reduces a major source of corrupt spoils, and striking at these privileges diminishes the attractiveness of the official unions and stimulates the rise of independent unions. Not only does this strain the prevailing corporatist model, but as the number of unions expands, corruption becomes a less applicable means of controlling labor and labor organizations.

Sixth, by pursuing its new model of economic development, the state places itself in a weaker ideological position than ever before. Not only is the philosophy embodied in the GATT contrary to the authoritarian-corporatist model of the Mexican state, but its reliance on the private sector tends to tilt the ideological balance toward business. Asking the private sector to lead the recovery by promoting export manufacturing, for instance, strengthens the private sector's position to make demands on the government. Both the state and the private sector recognize that the success of this new economic model requires economic efficiencies in the production and marketing of Mexican products on the world market. The opportunities created under "political capitalism" may make the customary forms of corruption inconsistent with this model. For example, 10 percent overhead for bribes or inefficient sweetheart contracts for union leaders defeats the tenets of the economic strategy.

Finally, the renewed emphasis on democracy under De la Madrid and Salinas affects corruption, forcing the PRI to select more popular candidates for political positions; widespread corruption among their ranks is costly in electoral terms. By contrast, attacking corruption is a means of enhancing the party's popular appeal and that of the president. The two major reasons given for Salinas's replacement by decree of various state governors in 1988–89 centered on their unpopularity with the voters and the approaching elections.[48] In pursuit of this strategy, an effort has been made to marginalize corrupt officials from what many see as the new "reformed" party. It is expected (wished?) that the two processes will proceed apace, that as the party "reforms" by attacking the abuses of the past, its popularity will increase among the people.

As a consequence of these trends, business, professional organizations, and opposition parties attained a new maturity in their organizational capacities and hence their ability to press for an end to corruption that works to their detriment. This is reflected in the struggles against corruption in the 1980s. In 1981, for example, a confederation of transport organizations was instrumental in denouncing the sale of tags to taxi drivers in Mexico City, and in 1985 leaders from a number of professional organizations in Guadalajara united to orchestrate a massive campaign against police corruption.[49] According to the president of the Hotel Association in Puebla, one of the group's major priorities has been to pressure government for better-trained inspectors in an effort to end corrupt practices. The results have been excellent: the days when inspectors might not even enter the hotel or restaurant but would await their bribe outside, this official stated, have passed. Likewise, within the press, some credit the persistence of the Democratic Journalists Union (UPD) in pressuring the government in the Buendía case.[50]

Clearly, the recent changes are affecting the state-society balance, reducing the state's control over mobility opportunities. With "critics of the regime now hav[ing] . . . an alternative to the politics of cooptation,"[51] social organizations are in a better position to check the abuses of state power and state officials have a smaller power base to exploit. Like an adjustment process, the crisis of corruption may therefore reflect these growing demands mobilized through opposition parties, independent labor unions, and even anticorruption organizations for higher levels of bureaucratic professionalism and greater accountability.

But though these signs suggest a more constrained role for corruption in the system, the changes also present the PRI-led regime with a fundamental paradox. Corruption may appear contrary to the new economic reforms and the invigoration of elections, but attacking corruption strikes at the very heart of the political machine, increasingly alienating those segments of the party that have traditionally run the electoral contests and helped maintain worker and popular discipline. This is dangerous for a variety of reasons. For one, continued labor discipline is pivotal because of the economic crisis; a more independent labor or peasant sector would render pursuit of the economic program difficult. Indeed, experience shows the importance of labor's support during periods of crisis.[52]

Second, the party's political stalwarts are critical in marshaling the electoral resources of the traditional political machine. Although much weaker than in the past, this political infrastructure plays a crucial role in the electoral life of the party; the *políticos* are far more adept at mass mobilization and negotiations than the technocrats.[53] Thus attacking the corruption that has helped wed the disparate party interests could disrupt the machine precisely at a juncture of greatest need.

Third, and perhaps most significant, these actors are crucial in endowing the PRI's revolutionary claims with credibility. Without the labor and peasant sectors incorporated into the ranks of the party and echoing the party's revolutionary agenda, the party's social-nationalistic legitimacy may be threatened. Yet "the combination of a persistent anti-labor bias in government economic policy and renewed attacks by political technocrats might lead major segments of the labor movement to question the continued viability of the state-labor alliance."[54] This danger—represented in part by attacks on the traditional privileges and corruption of the party veterans and thereby forcing a wedge between the PRI's revolutionary legacy and the patronage system that helped the party sustain it—is exacerbated by the new role of elections and the emergence of the leftist-nationalist alliance in the Cárdenas-led front (as of 1988, the PRD). Challenging the PRI on its own terms (who is the true heir to the ideals of the Mexican Revolution?), the PRD threatens to "steal" the legacy of the revolution. Although voters summarily rejected corrupt labor leaders at the polls in 1988, they may have been rejecting corruption and not the interests of labor.[55] Thus relinquishing key party professionals could mean the loss of a major mobilizational device (the revolutionary credentials of the regime).

The danger thus persists that the party could lose its internal integrity before there are assurances that the "reformed" party can muster majority support: the strategy, in short, could backfire, costing the party its control over the government. As Cornelius et al. argue: "The string of defeats that an unreformed and 'unprotected' party would undoubtedly suffer could provoke a dangerous confrontation between reformers and hardliners within the regime."[56]

Recent experience reveals the inherent dangers in this strategy. De la Madrid's anticorruption drive and his electoral openings faced enormous pressures; they eventually succumbed to the forces of reaction. The costs of exposing corruption eventually became counterproductive, leading to the campaign's deterioration, and a policy of allowing "transparent elections" during the early years was reversed following rapid electoral gains by the PAN. The election of Salinas himself, despite the promises of clean elections, also rested on old methods and the old guard: "Without the caciques and the rest of the 'dinosaurs' who mobilize the vote and manipulate it in the traditional way, it would have been very difficult for Salinas to win." In fact, Salinas's "margin of victory came from the most traditional, underdeveloped areas and the most marginalized segments of the population," those most susceptible to the methods and exhortations of the traditional elite. Although Cornelius et al. contend that the fraud of the presidential election showed the Salinas group's (the "reformers") "*lack* of control over the PRI apparatus and key functionaries," the highest electoral authority at the time (the interior secretary) was rewarded, not punished, with a cabinet-level appointment in the Salinas administration.[57]

This dynamic paradox manifests itself in a strange, often intriguing mixture of reform and reaction: signs that the PRI has begun to reform and adapt to the electoral challenge mixed with clear signs of old-time methods of fraud, corruption, and repression. Thus though Salinas exhorts that "the PRI has proved its democratic will,"[58] local elections such as those in Michoacán, Durango, Oaxaca, and other places in 1988–89 evidenced blatant fraud and manipulation; though the PAN has made unmatched electoral strides in some areas such as Baja California, simultaneous elections in Michoacán are touted as "the most fraudulent electoral process in history."[59] Even a spokesperson for the PAN complained that "there has been so much forgery on both sides that it is very difficult to say [who won and in which districts]."[60]

The colliding forces of this paradox emerge in different patterns. In some cases, they may extend from a common point. In the electoral arena, for instance, many feel that these contradictory signals (promises of clean elections followed by fraud) emerge from the top. As Luis Javier Garrido notes: "The Interior Secretary . . . has been converted into the maximum authority in the preparation, development, organization and execution of the electoral fraud."[61] Yet in other instances, the contradictory tendencies seem to flow from disparate locations. The broadened freedoms of press ushered in under De la Madrid, for example, met a wave of violence that resulted in the death of thirty-two journalists, including Manuel Buendía.

In sum, corruption historically enhanced the PRI's ability to "buy" and maintain the support of key sectoral leaders. This permitted it to pursue a successful mixture of coercion and co-optation to discipline and incorporate labor and peasant sectors, which lent credibility to the party's "revolutionary" credentials and helped keep the left divided.[62] Attacking this corruption directly or fostering a system that discourages it significantly alters the equation.

Conclusion

The three sets of factors or theses highlighted to account for the crisis of corruption are not mutually exclusive. It is plausible that although economic crisis and the Moral Renovation campaign prompted a greater awareness of corruption, much of that concern may have stemmed from the rise of oil- and drug-related corruption. Since that time though, the economic and political dynamics have significantly altered the picture, transforming other components of the system, including corruption. It is possible that if economic prosperity is restored, the historical system may prevail and the nature (frequency, type, functions) of corruption in Mexico will continue as in the past. Yet the changes of the 1980s have been significant, and a complete return to the past is highly unlikely. Still, the degree of fundamental change—and therefore its impact on corruption—remains a matter of contention, debate, and, within Mexico, often struggle and violence.

Conclusion

As the preceding discussion has shown, past anti-corruption campaigns have demonstrated sincere intentions and a variety of reforms. The law mandates financial disclosures and competitive bidding for public works contracts, yet past reforms have been ignored, dismantled, and insufficient. As Amitai Etzioni notes, "reforms cannot succeed on their own or be advanced against historical trends."[1]

One major thrust of this study has been to treat corruption as involving broad, structural factors and historical forces. It was argued, for example, that the currents unleashed in the 1980s may prove to have a greater impact on corruption than all the reform efforts of the past. But in addition, the analysis underscores other broad areas of change that could bridle corruption in Mexico. Some of these, as well as the inherent, deceptive danger in discussing reforms, merit brief attention.

First, reducing the scope and role of personalistic politics in Mexico is crucial in shrinking the environment in which corruption flourishes. An increase in public policy debates and other activities of government, opening the closed doors, and permitting greater public scrutiny of official processes would clearly have such an impact. Generally, the more public government affairs become, the less corrupt they can be.

Enhancing the autonomy of the state's subsystems would also reduce the likelihood of corruption. This could be pursued, for instance, by creating an effective civil service system or merit system or opening up grass-roots political involvement. Such reforms would cripple the centralization of recruitment and thereby temper the loyalty patterns that currently prevail. Strengthening the autonomy and role of Congress or democratizing corporate organizations would be steps in this direction. Strengthening social organizations would also impinge on corruption. This could be done by reducing the tutelary role of the state and lessening the dependency of social organizations on the state or by enhancing popular input into the organizations themselves. Not only must businesses or unions articulate demands on the government, but such organizations must be structurally responsive to the demands of their constituents. Tying the fate of leaders of social organizations to criteria internal to the group rather than those determined by the state would greatly inhibit current patterns of corruption.

The second major thrust of this study, however, concerns the importance of incorporating corruption into the broader perspective of Mexican politics, and herein lies the inherent danger in addressing the issue of reforming corruption. Structural reforms do not operate in a vacuum, and corruption is neither an isolated problem nor Mexico's only problem. Pressures reducing corruption may hold disastrous consequences for the functioning and stability of the system. Moreover, the reforms designed to attack corruption could trigger and expose other, more destabilizing and perhaps irreconcilable problems. Curbing corruption could jeopardize the pragmatic and accommodating agreement that has long united the elite; reducing centralized political control or corporatist control, despite certain benefits, could result in uncontrolled political mobilizations and unmediated demands that could be more difficult to contend with than corruption itself; closing the channels of accommodation forged by corruption could rechannel demands into more public arenas, igniting political conflict and triggering divisive ideological debates. Indeed, these linkages and ramifications make the implementation of any anticorruption plan complex and the incorporation of corruption into a broad overall perspective vital.

As a systemic feature, corruption in Mexico influences the nature, content, and direction of future reform, just as the other reforms affect corruption. Huntington contends that corruption is a substitute for reform; Johnson avers that it undermines reform.[2] Either way, given the magnitude of the political and economic difficulties Mexico faces, it is likely that, by undermining authority and fostering distrust, a legacy of political corruption may compromise and erode the government's ability to respond. Economic stagnation and slow democratic progress further feed the flames of frustration and distrust built on years of unfulfilled promises and widespread corruption.

The Mexican political system has long been considered something of an enigma; the general inattention to political corruption and failure to incorporate it into a comprehensive analysis may partially account for this. As history and the foregoing analysis make clear, corruption has played a crucial role in the operation and stability of the Mexican system and, even amid the momentous changes of the 1980s and the challenges of the 1990s, retains its saliency today: it is a major political issue and force, attracting great attention from government, the opposition, and the general populace; it remains a crucial component of Mexican politics.

Rather than decay or decadence from a once wholesome state, corruption is a manifestation and constant reminder of the imperfections of governments generally to achieve the goals they embody. This inquiry has tried to underscore structural factors shaping that chasm between desire and deed and to explore the somewhat paradoxical political role of corruption. Some questions have been answered and others fashioned, but it is clear that just as the polity is incomplete without corruption, so too is our understanding of it.

Appendix

Collection and Coding of News Articles

Articles on political corruption in the Mexican press were identified using two methods, although the type of information retrieved followed the same basic format. For the years 1970, 1971, 1972, and 1974, a random sample of fifty-two editions per year of *El Excélsior* and *El Nacional* were reviewed; articles for the years 1976 to 1984 were located using the index *Información Sistemática*, which normally provided the relevant information through abstracts or led to a direct search of the news source.

The collection and recording of the data followed simple rules on the type of information sought, some with open-ended categories. Coding of data, however, involved more rigorous guidelines and the continuous collapsing of categories. More than one person participated in the collection and recording stage, but only one person actually coded the data. Besides the newspaper and date, the following variables and values were recorded:

1. Type of report. Reports were grouped into three categories: case, general denunciation, and reform. A case referred to a specific incident of corruption; a general denunciation would employ a more ambiguous tone in discussing corruption even in a particular area of the government; and a reform article detailed promises, actual reforms, or recommendations directed toward reducing corruption.

2. Type of Corruption. Recording the type of corrupt act relied

basically on the nomenclature employed in the article itself (bribery, extortion, nepotism, and so on). This category was open-ended. Later, coding revealed fourteen different types of corruption. Hence categories with very few entries were collapsed, as were categories sharing certain analytic characteristics.

3. Bureaucratic location. Also an open-ended category, bureaucratic location entailed merely noting the government agency or department mentioned in the report. As with type of corruption, the coding revealed an unmanageable set of agencies and departments that were later broken down by functional area, including Congress, the attorney general, the same bureaucratic agency, and so on, as shown in Table 3.2.

4. Geographic location. Although all the articles came from the Mexico City press, the location of the corrupt act was recorded following regional categories used by the Mexican government. These data ultimately were not used because of the overwhelming bias of the reports relating to the central region and the Federal District.

5. Denouncing party. This variable referred to the source of the information on a particular case or the author of the denunciation or reform. This was also recorded as an open-ended category, and the classifications were eventually collapsed following functional area, as was done with bureaucratic location.

6. Tone. An article's tone was classified as either positive or negative. Articles mentioning government action interpreted as contributing to the fight against corruption (e.g., investigation, prosecution, rhetoric, or reforms) were coded as positive; articles describing or decrying corruption, depicting it more as a problem with government inaction, were deemed negative in tone.

7. Problem perception. This variable dealt with the underlying and often unarticulated nature of the problem of corruption as depicted in the article. Three values were identified: personalistic, systemic, or citizenry. Articles dealing with specific cases or any indication that the root of the problem lay with specific individuals were coded as personalistic; articles depicting corruption as a flaw or ingredient in the system and not individual idiosyncrasies were considered systemic; and articles that emphasized inaction or referred to any other characteristics of the people as the root of the problem were coded under the citizenry category.

The Survey

The public opinion survey poll was carried out in the cities of Puebla and Huejotzingo on March 1, 1986, and Mexico City on March 8, 1986. Students from the Universidad de las Américas, Puebla, conducted the interviews as an optional assignment in a Comparative Politics class. An orientation session acquainted the students with the overall design of the study and the proper techniques and procedures to be followed while administering the questionnaire. All but one of the some thirty-four students participating were Mexican nationals. Being a non-Mexican, I did not administer the questionnaire myself except during a pretesting stage.

Specific sites in the three cities were selected nonrandomly in an effort made to include a good mix of lower-, middle-, and upper-class public areas. The locations included markets, parks, shopping centers, shopping malls, *centros*, and subway stations. Teams of two to three students covered each area. Given the problem of follow-up checks, however, supervisors were assigned to each locale to ensure that proper procedures were being followed. In most cases, the students were unacquainted with the supervisors, who eventually made themselves known. Fortunately, very few irregularities were uncovered, although some forty interviews were eventually excluded for various reasons.

Survey Questionnaire (English translation follows)

1. En una escala de 1 a 7, ordene Ud. los siguientes problemas que tiene México del más importante (como 1) al menos importante (como 7).
   —la crísis en centroamérica
   —inflación
   —corrupción

—relaciones con los Estados Unidos
—la deuda externa
—producción agrícola
—el desempleo

2. En otra escala de 1 a 7, ordene Ud. las siguientes causas de la crísis económica de la más importante (como 1) a la menos importante (como 7).

—bajos precios de petróleo
—la devaluación del peso
—relaciones con los Estados Unidos
—la deuda externa
—corrupción
—bajo nivel de productividad
—las exigencias sindicales

3. Ud. cree que el gobierno hace lo correcto: todo el tiempo, muchas veces, pocas veces o casi nunca.

4. ¿Diría Ud. que el gobierno se maneja por los intereses de unos pocos cuidandose a si mismo, o que los maneja para el beneficio del pueblo?

5. ¿Generalmente, para arreglar un asunto con el gobierno ¿es necesario pagar una mordida: siempre, muchas veces, pocas veces o casi nunca?

6. El Presidente de la Madrid ha empeñado un programa de "Renovación Moral" desde que asumió el puesto. Generalmente, ¿cree Ud. que el programa ha aumentado la honestidad en el gobierno: mucho, un poco o casi nada?

7. Parte del programa de "Renovación Moral" incluye la investigación y consignación de funcionarios. ¿Cree Ud. que el gobierno actual está realizando: demasiada, suficiente o muy poca acción de este tipo?

8. En una escala de 1 a 7, ordene Ud. las siguientes situaciones del crímen más grave (como 1) al menos grave (como 7).

—un trabajador llega a su trabajo sólo para cobrar
—un funcionario toma dinero del gobierno

—un funcionario da un trabajo en el gobierno a un familiar

—un criminal compra su libertad

—una persona da una mordida para tramitar un asunto burocrático

—un funcionario toma una decisión gubernamental para beneficiar a su negocio particular

—una persona da una mordida al policía para evitar una infracción

9. En otra escala de 1 a 7, ordene Ud. las mismas acciones de la mas cómun (como 1) a la menos común (como 7).

—un trabajador llega a su trabajo sólo para cobrar

—un funcionario toma dinero del gobierno

—un funcionario da un trabajo en el gobierno a un familiar

—un criminal compra su libertad

—una persona da una mordida para tramitar un asunto burocrático

—un funcionario toma una decisión gubernamental para beneficiar a su negocio particular

—una persona da una mordida al policía para evitar una infracción

10. En su opinión, los reportajes de corrupción en México son: ¿exagerados, suficientes o insuficientes?

11. ¿A qué se dedica Ud.?

12. ¿Dentro de cuál categoría se ubica su ingreso mensual?

A. hasta $50,000

B. de $50,000 a $100,000

C. de $100,000 a $150,000

D. de $150,000 a $200,000

E. de $200,000 a $300,000

F. más que $300,000

13. ¿Dentro de cuál categoría se ubica su más alto nivel de educación?

A. Primaria
B. Secundaria
C. Normal
D. Preparatoria
E. Universitario
F. Posgrado o Profesional
14. ¿Es Ud. miembro de un partido político? ¿Cuál? *Si contestan no, entonces: ¿Con cuál partido más se identifica?
15. ¿Es Ud. miembro de una organización social, económica, religiosa o cultural? ¿Cuáles?
16. ¿En las elecciones vota Ud.: siempre, la mayoría de las veces, pocas veces o casi nunca?
17. ¿Sigue Ud. los acontecimientos políticos y gubernamentales regularmente, de vez en cuando, o casi nunca?
18. ¿Cuántos años tiene?
Anota el sexo M o F

English Translation of Survey Questionnaire

1. On a scale from 1 to 7, rank the following problems facing Mexico from the most important (as 1) to the least important (as 7).
—the crisis in Central America
—inflation
—corruption
—relations with the United States
—the foreign debt
—agricultural production
—unemployment
2. On another scale from 1 to 7, rank the following causes of the economic crisis from the most important (as 1) to the least important (as 7).
—low petroleum prices
—the devaluation of the peso

—relations with the United States
—the external debt
—corruption
—low level of productivity
—the demands of labor unions

3. Do you believe the government does the correct thing all the time, much of the time, rarely, or almost never?[1]

4. Would you say the government is driven by the interests of a few looking after themselves or that it is run for the benefit of all the people?

5. Generally, to conclude a matter with the government, is it necessary to pay a bribe always, much of the time, rarely, or almost never?

6. President De la Madrid has undertaken a program of "Moral Renovation" since taking office. Generally, do you believe the program has increased honesty in government a lot, a little, or almost none?

7. Part of the "Moral Renovation" program includes the investigation and prosecution of public officials. Do you believe the current government is doing too much, enough, or very little of this type of action?

8. On a scale from 1 to 7, rank the following situations from the most serious crime (as 1) to the least serious (as 7).

—a worker arrives at his job only to receive his pay
—a public official takes money from the government
—a public official gives a job in the government to a member of his family
—a criminal buys his freedom
—a person gives a bribe to process a bureaucratic matter
—a public official makes a government decision to benefit his own private business
—a person gives a bribe to the police to avoid a traffic citation

9. On another scale from 1 to 7, rank these same situations from the most common (as 1) to the least common (as 7).

—a worker arrives at his job only to receive his pay

—a public official takes money from the government

—a public official gives a job in the government to a member of his family

—a criminal buys his freedom

—a person gives a bribe to process a bureaucratic matter

—a public official makes a government decision to benefit his own private business

—a person gives a bribe to the police to avoid a traffic citation

10. In your opinion, are the reports of corruption in Mexico exaggerated, sufficient, or insufficient?

11. What is your occupation?

12. Within which of the categories does your monthly income fall?

    A. to 50,000 pesos

    B. from 50,000 to 100,000 pesos

    C. from 100,000 to 150,000 pesos

    D. from 150,000 to 200,000 pesos

    E. from 200,000 to 300,000 pesos

    F. over 300,000

13. Within which of the categories does your highest level of education fall?

    A. Elementary

    B. Junior High School

    C. Normal School

    D. Senior High School

    E. College

    F. Graduation or Professional School

14. Are you a member of a political party? If so, which one? If not, with which party do you most identify?

15. Are you a member of a social, economic, religious, or cultural organization? Which ones?

16. In the elections, do you vote always, most of the time, rarely, or almost never?

17. Do you follow political and government affairs regularly, occasionally, or almost never?

18. What is your age?

Note male or female respondent.

Elite Interviews

The elite interviews took one of two formats: an oral interview or a written set of open-ended questions. Although the oral method was strongly preferred and desired, the written format was developed to allow respondents the opportunity to answer the questions at their convenience. By and large, the written responses proved far less in-depth than hoped for.

The questions raised during the oral face-to-face interviews were similar to the written ones, although they provided only a basic guide for the interview. The following questions were broadly worded so as to elicit general opinions on corruption. The oral interviews were followed up by more specific questions relating to the interviewee's area and responses. In both, the respondents were advised of the scholarly intent of the interview or questionnaire and assured anonymity.

The written questionnaire included the following questions:

1. What do you think about the efforts of President Miguel de la Madrid in his program of "Moral Renovation"? What steps have you taken in your area to support the president's efforts?

2. To what point do you consider corruption a national problem? In what sectors of society is it most pronounced?

3. Generally, what do you consider to be the principal causes of corruption in Mexico? In addition to those things mentioned earlier, what reforms are needed to deal with the problem?

4. In your specific area, what problems of this type are most evident?

5. In your opinion, what are the consequences, both positive and negative, of corruption in Mexico?

Such interviews were conducted with a member of Punto Crítico and journalist, April 19, 1986, Mexico City; a nonactive member of the Mexican Foreign Service, currently an academician, May 19, 1986, Puebla; a aide to the attorney general of Puebla (written response); an officer of the Federal Judicial Police (written response); an official of CANACINTRA of Puebla, May 22, 1986, Puebla; an official of the Association of Hotels of Puebla, May 22, 1986, Puebla; an official of Consejo de Junta de Mejoramiento, May 22, 1986, Puebla; an official of Consejo de Coordinación Empresariel de Puebla, May 22, 1986, Puebla; an official of CONCANACO, May 23, 1986, Puebla; an official of the Social Security Institute (IMSS) (written response); and a lawyer for Controlaría, May 9, 1986, Mexico City.

Notes

Introduction

1. See Carl J. Friedrich, *The Pathology of Politics: Violence, Betrayal, Corruption, Secrecy and Propaganda* (New York: Harper & Row, 1972).

2. Quoted in James Nelson Goodsell, "Mexicans Speak out against Government Corruption," *Christian Science Monitor,* October 6, 1982, p. 1.

3. See Miguel Cabildo, "Durazo obliga a su personal al entregarle el producto de sus mordidas," *Proceso* 386 (May 26, 1984): 16–17; and José González González *Lo Negro del Negro Durazo* (México: Posada, 1983).

4. See *Mexico City News,* November 14, 1985.

5. Leon Lazaroff, "Adiós DI or Is It Only hasta luego?" *Mexico Journal,* July 10, 1989, p. 7.

6. See, for example, Joel Brinkley, "Mexico and the Narcotics Traffic: Growing Strain in US Relations," *New York Times,* October 20, 1986, p. 4.

7. Alan Riding, "Mexico Police: Symbol of Corruption?" *New York Times,* February 13, 1983, p. 10.

8. Quoted in *Mexico Journal* 2, no. 35 (June 26, 1989): 14.

9. See *El Universal,* January 5, 1976, p. 1; and *Excélsior,* March 11, 1976, p. 28.

10. See Jack Anderson, "Mexican Wheels Are Lubricated by Official Oil," *Washington Post*, May 14, 1984, p. 11B; and Anderson, "Mexico Makes Its Presidents Millionaires," *Washington Post*, May 15, 1984, p. 15C.

11. William K. Murray, "Prospects for the Moral Renovation Campaign," unpublished paper (Glendale, Ariz.: American Graduate School of International Management, 1984).

12. Lola Romanucci-Ross, *Conflict, Violence and Morality in a Mexican Village* (Palo Alto, Calif.: National Press Books, 1973), p. 117.

13. See *Mexico City News*, January 24, 1986, p. 4.

14. William Stockton, "Bribes Are Called a Way of Life for the Mexicans," *New York Times*, October 25, 1986, p. 3.

15. See *Unomasuno*, December 4, 1985.

16. Eric Wolf, *Sons of the Shaking Earth* (Chicago: University of Chicago Press, 1959).

17. Cited in Edwin Lieuwen, *Arms and Politics in Latin America* (New York: Praeger, 1960), p. 102.

18. Alan Knight, *The Mexican Revolution*, vol. 2: *Counter-Revolution and Reconstruction* (New York: Cambridge University Press, 1986), p. 10; Paul J. Vanderwood, *Disorder and Progress: Bandits, Police and Mexican Development* (Lincoln: University of Nebraska Press, 1981).

19. Quoted in John W. Sloan, *Public Policy in Latin America: A Comparative Survey* (Pittsburgh: University of Pittsburgh Press, 1984), p. 147.

20. Frank Tannenbaum, *Mexico: The Struggle for Peace and Bread* (New York: Knopf, 1950), p. 79.

21. *El Nacional*, June 7, 1972, p. 5.

22. *El Excélsior*, February 11, 1976.

Chapter 1

1. For a sampling of the debate over definition see Arnold J. Heidenheimer, ed., *Political Corruption: Readings in Comparative Analysis* (New York: Holt, Rinehart and Winston, 1970), pp. 3–9; and Harry Holloway and Frank S. Meyers, "Refining the Definition of Cor-

ruption: Reflections from an Oklahoma Study" (paper presented at the Southwestern Political Science Association meeting, Houston, Texas, March 20–23, 1985).

2. Tevfik F. Nas, Albert C. Price, and Charles T. Weber, "A Policy-Oriented Theory of Corruption," *American Political Science Review* 80 (1986): 108.

3. George Benson, *Political Corruption in America* (Lexington, Mass.: Lexington Books, 1978), p. xiii.

4. H. A. Brasz, "Some Notes on the Sociology of Corruption," *Sociologica Neerlandica* 1 (Autumn 1963): 111–17; rpt. as "The Sociology of Corruption," in Heidenheimer, ed., *Political Corruption*, p. 42.

5. Heidenheimer, ed., *Political Corruption*, pp. 3–9.

6. Arnold Rogow and Harold Lasswell, *Power, Corruption and Rectitude* (Englewood Cliffs, N.J.: Prentice-Hall, 1963), p. 132, depict the common interest as a rough criterion to define corruption.

7. Omotunde E. G. Johnson, "An Economic Analysis of Corrupt Government with Special Application to Less Developed Countries," *Kylos* 28 (1975): 47.

8. Corruption is thus in a class of behavior referred to as patron-client relations or clientelism. See Rene Lemarchand, "Comparative Political Clientelism: Structure, Process and Optic," in *Political Clientelism, Patronage and Development*, ed. S. N. Eisenstadt and Rene Lemarchand (Beverly Hills: Sage, 1981), p. 15.

9. Brasz, "Sociology," p. 43.

10. Lawrence W. Sherman, *Scandal and Reform: Controlling Police Corruption* (Berkeley and Los Angeles: University of California Press, 1978), p. 120.

11. Gabriel Ben-Dor, "Corruption, Institutionalization, and Political Development: The Revisionist Theses Revisited," *Comparative Political Studies* 7 (1974): 69.

12. Stanislav Andreski, "Kleptocracy of Corruption as a System of Government," in *The African Predicament* (New York: Atherton, 1968), pp. 92–109; rpt. as "Kleptocracy as a System of Government in Africa," in Heidenheimer, ed., *Political Corruption*, p. 352.

13. Gaetano Mosca, *The Ruling Class* (New York: McGraw-Hill, 1939).

14. Oscar Oszlak, "The Historical Formation of the State in Latin America: Some Theoretical and Methodological Guidelines for Its Study," *Latin American Research Review* 16, no. 2 (1981): 15.

15. Johnson, "Economic Analysis," p. 48.

16. Joel S. Migdal, "A Model of State-Society Relations," in *New Directions in Comparative Politics*, ed. Howard J. Wiarda (Boulder, Colo.: Westview Press, 1985), p. 46.

17. A sample of typologies differentiates corruption according to degree of deviance in elite and mass opinions (see Heidenheimer, ed., *Political Corruption*, pp. 26–28; and Holloway and Meyers, "Refining the Definition"), the bureaucratic location of the officials involved (upper level/lower levels; bureaucratic/electoral), the flow of political resources (Johnson, "Economic Analysis"), the frequency of the political exchange (Robert Dowse, "Conceptualizing Corruption," rev. of *Society and Bureaucracy in Contemporary Ghana*, by Robert M. Price, *Government and Opposition* 12 [1977]: 244; Michael Johnston, "The Political Consequences of Corruption: A Reassessment," *Comparative Politics* 18, no. 4 [1986]: 465–66), the nature of the political favor (V. O. Key, Jr., *Techniques of Political Graft in the United States* [Chicago: University of Chicago Libraries, 1936], pp. 386–401; rpt. as "Techniques of Political Graft," in Heidenheimer, ed., *Political Corruption*, pp. 46–48; J. G. Peters and S. Welch, "Political Corruption in America: Search for Definitions and a Theory or If Political Corruption Is in Mainstream of American Politics, Why Is It Not in the Mainstream of American Politics Research," *American Political Science Review* 72 [1978]: 974–84), or the underlying motivation of the corrupt act (Andreski, "Kleptocracy as a System," p. 352).

18. For a rich analysis of the relationship between bureaucratic factors and corruption see Susan Rose-Ackerman, *Corruption: A Study in Political Economy* (New York: Academic Press, 1978).

19. Gunnar Myrdal, "Corruption: Its Causes and Effects," in *Asian Drama: An Enquiry into the Poverty of Nations* (New York: Twentieth Century Fund, 1968), 2:951–58; rpt. as "Corruption as a Hindrance to Modernization in South Asia," in Heidenheimer, ed., *Political Corruption*, p. 541.

20. Key, *Techniques*, pp. 46–48.

21. Migdal, "Model of State-Society Relations," p. 51.

22. See Anne Deysine, "Political Corruption: A Review of the Literature," *European Journal of Political Research* 8 (1980): 447–62.

23. Rogow and Lasswell, *Power,* and Rose-Ackerman, *Corruption,* contend that the concentration of power leads to its abuse, whereas Benson, *Political Corruption,* and James Q. Wilson, "Corruption: The Shame of the States," *Public Interest* 2 (1966): 28–38, rpt. in Heidenheimer, ed., *Political Corruption,* pp. 298–306, both argue that decentralized authority creates a greater number of access points through which corrupt influences can be exerted.

24. See Bert F. Hoselitz, "Levels of Economic Performance and Bureaucratic Structures," in Joseph La Palombara, ed., *Bureaucracy and Political Development* (Princeton: Princeton University Press, 1963), pp. 188–96, rpt. as "Performance Levels and Bureaucratic Structure," in Heidenheimer, ed., *Political Corruption,* pp. 76–81; Samuel P. Huntington, *Political Order in Changing Societies* (New Haven: Yale University Press, 1968), pp. 59–71; H. A. Brasz, "Some Notes," pp. 117–25, rpt. as "Administrative Corruption in Theory and Dutch Practice," in Heidenheimer, ed., *Political Corruption,* pp. 243–48; and W. Michael Reisman, *¿Remedios contra la corrupción?* trans. Mariluz Caso (México: Fondo de Cultura Económica, 1983), originally published as *Folded Lies: Bribery, Crusades and Reforms* (New York: Free Press, 1979).

25. See Roger D. Hansen, *The Politics of Mexican Development* (Baltimore: Johns Hopkins Press, 1971); Merle Kling, "Towards a Theory of Power and Political Instability in Latin America," *Western Political Science Quarterly* 9, no. 1 (1956): 21–35; M. McMullan, "A Theory of Corruption," *Sociological Review* 9, no. 2 (1961): 181–201; James C. Scott, *Comparative Political Corruption* (Englewood Cliffs, N.J.: Prentice-Hall, 1972); and Wolf, *Sons of the Shaking Earth.*

26. On unsatisfied demand for government services as a cause of corruption see Andreski, "Kleptocracy as a System," pp. 346–60; Norberto Quezada, "Un modelo del comportamiento corrupto," in *Cinco ensayos sobre la corrupción* (Santiago: Universidad Madre y Maestra, 1980); and Robert T. Tilman, "Emergence of Black Market Bureaucracy: Administration, Development and Corruption in the New States," *Public Administration Review* 28 (1968): 440–42, rpt. in Heidenheimer, ed., *Political Corruption,* pp. 62–64.

27. On the role of accountability (and democracy) in discouraging corruption see Johnson, "Economic Analysis"; McMullen, "Theory of Corruption"; Nas, Price, and Weber, "Policy-Oriented Theory"; and Rose-Ackerman, *Corruption*.

28. See, for example, Edward C. Banfield, *The Moral Basis of a Backward Society* (New York: Free Press, 1958); Huntington, *Political Order*; McMullan, "Theory of Corruption"; and Ronald E. Wraith and Edgar Simpkins, *Corruption in Developing Countries* (London: Allen and Unwin, 1963).

29. See, for example, Amitai Etzioni, *Capital Corruption: The New Attack on American Democracy* (San Diego: Harcourt, 1984); Peters and Welch, "Political Corruption"; and Michael Pinto-Duschinsky, "Theories of Corruption in American Politics" (paper presented at the annual meeting of the American Political Science Association, Chicago, 1976).

30. On how such a situation prevails in the United States, particularly how special interests penetrate government to forge unique patterns of corruption, see Etzioni, *Capital Corruption*.

31. John D. Nagle, *Introduction to Comparative Politics: Political System Performance in Three Worlds* (Chicago: Nelson-Hall, 1989), pp. 193–95. Scott, *Comparative Political Corruption*, p. ix, notes the low levels of corruption in North Vietnam; Maurice Zeitlin, *Revolutionary Politics and the Cuban Working Class* (Princeton: Princeton University Press, 1970), highlights the Cuban case.

32. On the issue of the functionality of corruption see José Velasco Abueva, "The Contribution of Nepotism, Spoils and Graft to Political Development," *East-West Center Review* 3 (1966): 45–54; David H. Bayley, "The Effects of Corruption in a Developing Country," *Western Political Quarterly* 19 (1966): 719–32, rpt. in Heidenheimer, ed., *Political Corruption*, pp. 521–33; Huntington, *Political Order*; Johnston "Political Consequences"; Nathaniel H. Leff, "Economic Development through Bureaucratic Corruption," *American Behavioral Scientist* 8, no. 3 (1964): 8–14, rpt. in Heidenheimer, ed., *Political Corruption*, pp. 510–20.

33. Nas, Price, and Weber, "Policy-Oriented Theory," p. 110.

34. See Huntington, *Political Order*, pp. 58–71; Leff, "Economic Development"; Joseph S. Nye, "Corruption and Political Develop-

ment: A Cost-Benefit Analysis," *American Political Science Review* 61 (1967): 417–27; and Scott, *Comparative Political Corruption.*

35. Myrdal, *Asian Drama.*

36. This quote is attributed to an anonymous reviewer of the journal *Corruption and Reform.*

37. Jorge Tomás Vera, "Capitalismo y corrupción," *Yucatán: Historia y Economía* 1, no. 4 (1977): 27.

38. On this function of corruption see Bruce E. Gronbeck, "The Rhetoric of Political Corruption: Sociolinguistic, Dialectical and Ceremonial Processes," *Quarterly Journal of Speech* 64 (1978): 155–72. See also Murray Edelman, *The Symbolic Uses of Politics* (Champaign-Urbana: University of Illinois Press, 1964); and Stephen D. Morris, "Corruption and the Mexican Political System," *Corruption and Reform* 2, no. 1 (1987): 3–15.

39. Others suggest that corruption's positive functions are dependent on its being maintained within certain limits. See Friedrich, *Pathology of Politics.*

Chapter 2

1. For concise overviews of Mexican politics see Lawrence E. Koslow and Stephen P. Mumme, "The Evolution of the Mexican Political System: A Paradigmatic Analysis," in *The Future of Mexico*, ed. Koslow (Tempe: Arizona State University Center for Latin American Studies, 1981), pp. 47–98; Daniel Levy and Gabriel Szekeley, *Mexico: Paradoxes of Stability and Change* (Boulder, Colo.: Westview Press, 1983); and Carolyn Needleman and Martin Needleman, "Who Rules Mexico? A Critique of Some Current Views of the Mexican Political Process," *Journal of Politics* 31, no. 4 (1969): 1011–34.

2. Martin C. Needler, "Problems in the Evaluation of the Mexican Political System," in *Contemporary Mexico: Papers of the IV International Congress of Mexican History*, ed. James W. Wilkie, Michael C. Meyer, and Edna Monzon de Wilkie (Berkeley and Los Angeles: University of California Press, 1976), p. 339.

3. Examples of analyses that portray the system as essentially democratic include William P. Glade, Jr., and Charles W. Anderson, *The*

Political Economy of Mexico (Madison: University of Wisconsin Press, 1963); Martin C. Needler, *Politics and Society in Mexico* (Albuquerque: University of New Mexico Press, 1971); Vincent L. Padgett, *The Mexican Political System* (Boston: Houghton Mifflin, 1966); and Robert E. Scott, *Mexican Government in Transition* (Urbana: University of Illinois Press, 1959). For authoritarian assessments see Bo Anderson and James Cockcroft, "Control and Cooptation in Mexican Politics," *International Journal of Comparative Sociology* 7 (1966): 11–28; Frank Brandenburg, *The Making of Modern Mexico* (Englewood Cliffs, N.J.: Prentice-Hall, 1964); Hansen, *Politics of Mexican Development*; Kenneth F. Johnson, *Mexican Democracy: A Critical View*, rev. ed. (New York: Praeger, 1984); Susan K. Purcell, *The Mexican Profit-Sharing Decision: Politics in an Authoritarian Regime* (Berkeley and Los Angeles: University of California Press, 1975); José Luis Reyna and Richard S. Weinert, eds., *Authoritarianism in Mexico* (Philadelphia: Institute for the Study of Human Issues, 1977); and Evelyn P. Stevens, *Protest and Response in Mexico* (Cambridge, Mass.: MIT Press, 1974).

4. See Purcell, *Mexican Profit-Sharing Decision*; and Dale Story, *Industry, the State and Public Policy in Mexico* (Austin: University of Texas Press, 1986).

5. See Merilee Serrill Grindle, *Bureaucrats, Politicians and Peasants in Mexico: A Case Study in Public Policy* (Berkeley and Los Angeles: University of California Press, 1977).

6. See Daniel Levy, "University Autonomy in Mexico: Implications for Regime Authoritarianism," *Latin American Research Review* 14, no. 3 (1979): 129–52.

7. See Gabriel Almond and Sidney Verba, *The Civic Culture: Political Attitudes and Democracy in Five Nations* (Princeton: Princeton University Press, 1963); John A. Booth and Mitchell A. Seligson, "The Political Culture of Authoritarianism in Mexico: A Re-Examination," *Latin American Research Review* 19, no. 1 (1984): 106–24; Kenneth M. Coleman, *Public Opinion in Mexico City about the Electoral System*, James Sprunt Series in History and Political Science, no. 53 (Chapel Hill: University of North Carolina Press, 1972); and Kenneth F. Johnson, "The 1980 Image-Index Survey of Latin American Political Democracy," *Latin American Research Review* 17, no. 3 (1982): 193–201.

8. Needler, "Problems in the Evaluation," p. 343.

9. See Charles L. Davis, "Toward an Explanation of Mass Support for Authoritarian Regimes: A Case Study of Political Attitudes in Mexico City" (Ph.D. dissertation, University of Kentucky, 1974).

10. Richard R. Fagen and William S. Tuohy, *Politics and Privilege in a Mexican City* (Stanford: Stanford University Press, 1972), p. 20; Padgett, *Mexican Political System,* pp. 60, 9; and Sol Sanders, *Mexico: Chaos on Our Doorstep* (Lanham, Md.: Madison, 1986), p. 19.

11. Lorenzo Meyer, "Historical Roots of the Authoritarian State in Mexico," in ed. José Luis Reyna and Richard S. Weinert (Philadelphia: Institute for the Study of Human Issues, 1977), p. 3.

12. The compatibility of the principle of no reelection with the other components of the legitimizing ideology is a matter of debate. One delegate to the Constitutional Convention in Querétaro, for example, pointed out that "the no re-election principle, as you all know, is not democratic" (quoted in Jorge Carpizo, "The No Re-election Principle in Mexico," *Mexican Forum* 3, no. 4 [1983]: 10). Brandenburg, *Making of Modern Mexico,* pp. 3–7, takes a different view, arguing that the principle of no reelection is the system's only deviation from a totally authoritarian regime.

13. On the centralization of authority see Grindle, *Bureaucrats;* and Purcell, *Mexican Profit-Sharing Decision.*

14. Antonio Ugalde, *Power and Conflict in a Mexican Community: A Study of Political Integration* (Albuquerque: University of New Mexico Press, 1970), p. 95.

15. On the power of the Mexican president see Brandenburg, *Making of Modern Mexico;* and Guillermo Kelley, "Politics and Administration in Mexico: Recruitment and Promotion of the Politico-Administrative Class," *Mexican Forum* 1, no. 4 (1981): 8–11.

16. For a review of Mexican corporatism see Anderson and Cockcroft, "Control and Cooptation"; Rose Spalding, "State Power and Its Limits: Corporatism in Mexico," *Comparative Political Studies* 14 (1981): 139–61; and Evelyn P. Stevens, "Comment: The Mexican Presidential Succession," *Journal of Interamerican Studies and World Affairs* 19, no. 1 (1977): 125–26.

17. Davis, "Toward an Explanation," p. 12.

18. Purcell and Purcell, "Nature of the Mexican State," p. 23.

19. Reyna and Weinert, eds., *Authoritarianism*, p. 161.

20. On the press see Stevens, *Protest and Response*.

21. See Norman Cox, "Changes in the Mexican Political System," in *Politics in Mexico*, ed. George Philip (London: Croom Helm, 1985), p. 43.

22. Meyer, "Historical Roots," p. 16.

23. See Fagen and Tuohy, *Politics*, p. 30; Padgett, *Mexican Political System*; and Scott, *Mexican Government*.

24. See John F. H. Purcell and Susan Kaufman Purcell, "Machine Politics and Socio-Economic Change in Mexico," in *Contemporary Mexico: Papers of the IV International Congress of Mexican History*, ed., James W. Wilkie, Michael C. Meyer, and Edna Monzon de Wilkie (Berkeley and Los Angeles: University of California Press, 1976), p. 354.

25. See Pablo González Casanova, *La democracia en México*, 14th ed. (México: Era, 1965).

26. State legislatures are similarly subservient to the state executive. See Ugalde, *Power and Conflict*, p. 106.

27. See Robert E. Biles, "The Position of the Judiciary in the Political Systems of Argentina and Mexico," *Lawyer of the Americas* 8, no. 2 (1980): 292–94.

28. On Mexican federalism and the power of state governors see Miguel Acosta Romero, "Mexican Federalism: Conception and Reality," *Public Administration Review* 42, no. 5 (1982): 399–404; and Lawrence S. Graham, *Politics in a Mexican Community*, Latin American Monograph Series 1, no. 35 (Gainesville: University of Florida Press, 1968).

29. Meyer, "Historical Roots," p. 12.

30. Enrique González Pedrero, governor of Tabasco, was named to head the Instituto de Estudios Políticos, Económicos y Sociales (IEPES) in early 1988; Francisco Gutiérrez Barrios was moved from the governorship of Veracruz to his position at Gobernación; Enrique Alvarez Félix, the governor of Jalisco, became attorney general; Luis Martínez Villicana, the unpopular governor of Michoacán, was removed because of the threat faced by the left in the state; Xicoténcatl Leyva Mortera of Baja California was transferred to a "nonexistent" job at the National Development Bank (NAFINSA) in early 1989 be-

cause of his reputation for corruption in a state also facing electoral challenge; and Mario Ramón Beteta was removed from his post in the state of Mexico. According to Jorge Casteñeda, Beteta's removal was an attempt by the PRI to bolster its support in the state for upcoming elections. See *Latin American Weekly Report* 89-3 (September 21, 1989): 8.

31. The best analyses of the personalistic dimension of Mexican politics are provided by Roderic Ai Camp, *The Making of a Government: Political Leaders in Modern Mexico* (Tucson: University of Arizona Press, 1984); Purcell and Purcell, "Nature of the Mexican State"; Peter H. Smith, *Labyrinths of Power: Political Recruitment in Twentieth-Century Mexico* (Princeton: Princeton University Press, 1979); and Laurence Whitehead, "Why Mexico Is Ungovernable—Almost," Working Paper Number 54 (Washington, D.C.: Wilson Center, 1979).

32. Purcell and Purcell, "Machine Politics," p. 357.

33. *Equipos* and *camarillas* refer to informal networks of politicians, like "old-buddy" or "good-old-boy" networks in the United States. Members of the groups assist one another in obtaining political appointments and favors. See, for example, Purcell and Purcell, "Nature of the Mexican State," p. 2.

34. Quoted in Cox, "Changes in the Mexican Political System," p. 31.

35. Guillermo de la Peña, *A Legacy of Promises: Agriculture, Politics and Ritual in the Morelos Highlands of Mexico* (Austin: University of Texas Press, 1981), p. 245.

36. Smith, *Labyrinths of Power.*

37. Wayne A. Cornelius, *Politics and the Migrant Poor in Mexico City* (Stanford: Stanford University Press, 1975).

38. See Ugalde, *Power and Conflict*, pp. 85, 182, and 89.

39. Ronfeldt cited in Purcell and Purcell, "Machine Politics," p. 352; see also David Ronfeldt, *Atencingo: The Politics of Agrarian Struggle in a Mexican Ejido* (Stanford: Stanford University Press, 1973); Dale Story, "Entrepreneurs and the State in Mexico: Examining the Authoritarian Thesis," Technical Papers Series no. 30 (Austin: University of Texas, 1980), p. 7.

40. See Anderson and Cockcroft, "Control and Cooptation."

41. On the co-optation of labor leaders see Evelyn P. Stevens,

"Legality and Extra-Legality in Mexico," *Journal of Interamerican Studies and World Affairs* 12 (1970): 71; for peasant organizations see Robert F. Adie, "Cooperation, Cooptation and Conflict in Mexican Peasant Organizations," *Interamerican Economic Affairs* 24, no. 3 (1970): 3–25.

42. Raymond Vernon, for instance, goes to great length to make the point, stating on consecutive pages: "Once again . . . it is well to distinguish substance from spirit" and "The distinction between form and substance needs to be emphasized once more, however" (*The Dilemma of Mexico's Development* [Cambridge, Mass.: Harvard University Press, 1963], pp. 125 and 126).

43. James Cockcroft, "Coercion and Ideology in Mexican Politics," in *Dependence and Underdevelopment: Latin America's Political Economy*, ed. Cockcroft et al. (Garden City, N.Y.: Doubleday Anchor Press, 1972), p. 259; Stevens, *Protest and Response*, p. 24; Smith, *Labyrinths of Power*, pp. 242–77.

44. Quoted in Davis, "Toward an Explanation," p. 49.

45. Hansen, *Politics of Mexican Development*, pp. 7–8; Coleman, "Public Opinion," p. 5.

46. Vernon, *Dilemma*, pp. 33–38; Perry Ballard, "El modelo liberal y la política práctica," *Historia Mexicana* 92, no. 23 (1974): 649–55.

47. Cockcroft, "Coercion and Ideology," p. 259.

48. See Fernando Pérez Correa, "Contradictions and Continuities in Mexican Constitutionalism," in *Mexico Today*, ed. Tommie Sue Montgomery (Philadelphia: Institute for the Study of Human Issues, 1982), p. 60.

49. See Anderson and Cockcroft, "Control and Cooptation"; and Stevens, "Legality and Extra-Legality," pp. 67 and 71.

50. A somewhat similar interpretation is offered by Whitehead, "Why Mexico Is Ungovernable."

51. Meyer, "Historical Roots," p. 5.

52. Camp, *Making of a Government*; Padgett, *Mexican Political System*, p. 74.

53. Cornelius, *Politics and the Migrant Poor*, p. 54.

54. See Almond and Verba, *Civic Culture*; Booth and Seligson, "Political Culture"; Cornelius, *Politics and the Migrant Poor*; and Davis, "Toward an Explanation."

55. Padgett, *Mexican Political System*, p. 61.

56. Davis, "Toward an Explanation," pp. 93 and 84.

57. Booth and Seligson, "Political Culture," pp. 119–20.

58. See Guy E. Poitras, "Welfare Bureaucracy and Clientele Politics in Mexico," *Administrative Science Quarterly* 18, no. 1 (1973): 18–26; and Grindle, *Bureaucrats*. On the "formally" centralized yet "informally" decentralized arrangement during Spanish colonialism see Mark Hanson, "Organizational Bureaucracy in Latin America and the Legacy of Spanish Colonialism," *Journal of Interamerican Studies and World Affairs* 16, no. 2 (1974): 199–219.

59. Meyer, "Historical Roots," p. 12; Fagen and Tuohy, *Politics and Privilege*, p. 28.

60. Fagen and Tuohy, *Politics and Privilege*, p. 18.

61. See John Kautsky, *Patterns of Modernizing Revolutions: Mexico and the Soviet Union*, Sage Professional Papers in Comparative Politics, Vol. 5, Ser. 01-156 (Beverly Hills: Sage, 1975), pp. 39–41.

62. See Martin C. Needler, ed., *Political Systems of Latin America*, 2d ed. (New York: Van Nostrand Reinhold, 1970), p. 9.

63. Claudio Lomnitz, "Compliance and Coalitions in the Mexican Government, 1917–1940," in *Five Centuries of Law and Politics in Central Mexico*, ed. Ronald Spores and Ross Hassig, Vanderbilt University Publication in Anthropology 30 (Nashville: Vanderbilt University, 1984), p. 176.

64. Susan Eckstein, *The Poverty of Revolution* (Princeton: Princeton University Press, 1977).

65. Cornelius, *Politics and the Migrant Poor*, p. 80.

66. Poitras ("Welfare Bureaucracy") found this to be the case in the Mexican social security administration.

67. Vernon, *Dilemma*, p. 126.

68. See Purcell, *Mexican Profit-Sharing Decision*.

Chapter 3

1. Martin Greenberg, *Bureaucracy and Development: A Mexican Case Study* (Lexington, Mass.: Heath Lexington, 1970), p. 112.

2. Hansen, *Politics of Mexican Development*, p. 78. See David

Brock, "To the Corrupt Go the Spoils for More Than Half a Century," *Insight*, October 5, 1987, p. 1; Smith, *Labyrinths of Power*, pp. 159– 87; Kelley, "Politics and Administration," p. 8.

3. See Ugalde, *Power and Conflict*, p. 98.

4. See Purcell and Purcell, "Nature of the Mexican State," pp. 24–25; and Greenberg, *Bureaucracy and Development*, p. 71.

5. Kelley, "Politics and Administration," p. 8.

6. Greenberg, *Bureaucracy and Development*, p. 71.

7. Quoted in Keith Rosenblaum, "Wall of Corruption Encircles Sonoran Capital," *Arizona Daily Star*, August 9, 1987, p. 1.

8. See *Unomasuno*, July 29, 1983, p. 5.

9. *El Sol*, March 24, 1983, p. 5B; *Excélsior*, September 12, 1976; see "Rechazan los priístas que se amplie la investigación del fraude bursátil," *Proceso* 642 (February 20, 1989): 28–29.

10. Statement by Raúl Cárdenas quoted in Elías Chávez, "La ley de responsibilidades, violatoria de la Constitución," *Proceso* 238 (May 25, 1981): 13.

11. *Unomasuno*, November 6, 1985.

12. *Información Sistemática*, July 1984, p. 37.

13. *Unomasuno*, November 6, 1985.

14. Ibid., August 2, 1979, p. 1, November 23, 1979, p. 27.

15. *La Prensa*, August 2, 1979, p. 21.

16. Ricardo Medina Macías, *Crónica del desengaño: Cátalogo de la corrupción* (México: Editorial Asociados, 1983), p. 38.

17. See *Universal*, August 15, 1980, p. 21; *Excélsior*, August 22, 1980, p. 1.

18. The case of Governor Biebrich was one of the major scandals of 1976. Having resigned following the violent eviction of peasants at San Isidro and San Ignacio Río Muerto in 1975, the former governor was later charged with fraud. The accusation was accompanied by an order to apprehend Biebrich and freeze 50 percent of his assets. The case polarized the state of Sonora. Many supported Biebrich's claim that the charges were politically motivated. After the state supreme court cleared Biebrich of certain charges and ordered the return of his properties, the state government appealed the case. Two years later, the supreme court ruled against Biebrich for illicit enrichment, although the fraud charges were never proven. Biebrich consistently

claimed that he had been the victim of political vengeance. See reports in *El Día*, January 4 and 9, 1976, July 1, 1980, p. 7; *El Universal*, January 5, 1976, February 23, 1978, p. 1; *Excélsior*, May 10, 1977, pp. 14 and 28; *Novedades*, February 24, 1978, p. 6; *La Prensa*, July 3, 1980, p. 3; *Unomasuno*, July 1, 1980, p. 2; and Gerardo Galarza, "Biebrich recupera algo lo que le arrebató el celo por sus éxitos," *Proceso* 386 (March 26, 1984): 13–15.

19. *Excélsior*, August 22, 1980, p. 1.

20. *El Día*, December 3, 1983, p. 3M.

21. Carlos Ramírez, "Las finanzas de PEMEX a punto de estallar, por corrupción e incapacidad," *Proceso* 238 (May 25, 1981): 6.

22. Ugalde, *Power and Conflict*, pp. 120–21.

23. *Excélsior*, November 22, 1977, p. 5.

24. James W. Wilkie, "The Dramatic Growth of Mexico's Economy and the Rise of Statist Government Budgetary Power, 1910–1982," *Mexican Forum* 5, no. 4 (1985): 37.

25. See Brock, "To the Corrupt Go the Spoils."

26. See Grindle, *Bureaucrats*, p. 3; and Sloan, *Public Policy*, p. 134.

27. Ben Ross Schneider, "Partly for Sale: Privatization and State Strength in Brazil and Mexico," *Journal of Interamerican Studies and World Affairs* 30, no. 4 (1988–89): 102.

28. Sloan, *Public Policy*, p. 129.

29. David A. Brading, "El estado en México en la época de los Habsburgos," *Historia Mexicana* 92, no. 23 (1974): 555; Hanson, "Organizational Bureaucracy," p. 203.

30. See Ramírez, "Finanzas de PEMEX," p. 6.

31. Interview with official of CANACINTRA, Puebla, Mexico, May 22, 1986.

32. Conclusion drawn from interview with official of the Consejo de Junta de Mejoramiento, a local business interest group, Puebla, Mexico, May 22, 1986. See also Smith, *Labyrinths of Power*, pp. 191–216.

33. Paul H. Lewis, "Development Strategies and the Decline of the Democratic Left in Latin America," in *The Continuing Struggle for Democracy in Latin America*, ed. Howard J. Wiarda (Boulder, Colo.: Westview Press, 1980), p. 191; Schneider, "Partly for Sale," p. 91.

34. Steven M. Rubin, *Mexico: Conditions and Risks for Business,*

Special Report 1103 (London: Economist Intelligence Unit, 1987), p. 92.

35. Ugalde, *Power and Conflict*, p. 100.

36. Interview with official of Consejo de Coordinación Empresarial, Puebla, Mexico, May 22, 1986; interview with official of Consejo de Junta de Mejoramiento.

37. Tannenbaum, *Mexico*, p. 99.

38. See *Unomasuno*, December 22, 1979, p. 7.

39. Among the countless reports of wrongdoing on the part of petroleum-related unions see those in *El Sol*, November 17, 1976; *El Día*, June 20, 1981, p. 2; *Universal*, September 4, 1983, p. 16; *Excélsior*, September 9, 1983, p. 21; and *Excélsior*, September 27, 1983, p. 1; *Latin American Regional Report* RM 89-02 (February 16, 1989): 6–7; and Salvador Corro, "Ofensiva final en Ciudad Madero, para acabar con todo vestigio quinista," *Proceso* 658 (June 12, 1989): 10–15.

40. *Mexico City News*, November 14, 1985.

41. See *Unomasuno*, September 14, 1981, p. 6; and *Excélsior*, April 5, 1971, p. 1.

42. Daniel Levy, "The Political Consequences of Changing Socialization Patterns," in *Mexico's Political Stability: The Next Five Years*, ed. Roderic Ai Camp (Boulder, Colo.: Westview Press, 1986), p. 32.

43. Interview with Rafael Rodríguez Castañeda, *Proceso*, November 3, 1981, pp. 6–9.

44. Stevens, *Protest and Response*, p. 44.

45. Interview with official of Consejo de Coordinación Empresarial.

46. See Sanders, *Mexico*, p. 27.

47. Marco Aurelio Carballo, "Enrique Florescano: La corrupción, forma de control político," *Proceso* 39 (August 1, 1977): 14–15.

48. See, for instance, Kling, "Towards a Theory of Power"; and Wolf, *Sons of the Shaking Earth*.

49. Hansen, *Politics of Mexican Development*, p. xiii.

50. Interview with leftist activist and journalist, Mexico City, April 19, 1986.

51. *Vuelta*, no. 276001 (May 1978): 5–9.

52. This view was expressed by an official of CANACINTRA, Puebla, Mexico, May 22, 1986.

53. *Vuelta*, no. 276001 (May 1978): 5–9.

54. Alan Riding, *Distant Neighbors: A Portrait of the Mexicans* (1984; rpt. New York: Vintage Books, 1984), p. 174.

55. On the importance of scandal as a social phenomenon see Graeme C. Moodie, "On Political Scandals and Corruption," *Government and Opposition* 15 (1980): 208–22.

56. Such scandals include those involving Biebrich (see note 18 above), Norgueda Otero, and the Flores Tapia. Norgueda Otero, the former governor of Guerrero, was arrested in August 1976 for a fraud of 18 million pesos and later found innocent of the charges (see *Excélsior*, August 6, 1976, p. 1, January 6, 1977, p. 10). Flores Tapia, the governor of Coahuila, was charged with "unexplained wealth" approaching 2 billion pesos. Although he was allowed to go free, many of his massive property holdings were confiscated by the state. Of the many articles and books documenting Flores Tapia's massive wealth acquired while he was governor see Miguel Cepeda, "En 13 años, Flores Tapia pasó de la quiebra a la riqueza," *Proceso* 240 (June 6, 1981): 21–24; Armando Castilla, *El caso de Flores Tapia* (Mexico: Grijalbo, 1982); and Medina Macías, *Crónica*.

57. The IMSS scandal centered around the discovery of clandestine laboratories and the involvement of officials in the illegal sale of medicines. The scandal touched off a debate on the issue of nationalizing the largely foreign-owned pharmaceutical industry. See *Excélsior*, February 9, 1977, p. 1; *El Universal*, February 13, 1977, p. 1; *Novedades*, February 16, 1977, p. 1.

58. The official accusation for extorting 500 million pesos in June 1977 set up a national manhunt for the director of the Bahia de Banderas Trust Fund, Alfredo Ríos Camarena. Meanwhile, reports revealed his lavish holdings and spending sprees. Following his extradition from Miami in 1978, Ríos Camarena eventually returned 11 million pesos and won conditional freedom while awaiting the results of repeatedly delayed appeals. See *Excélsior*, July 20, 1977, p. 1, January 3, 1978, p. 1, and July 26, 1977, p. 1; *Unomasuno*, March 17, 1978, p. 1; and Medina Macías, *Crónica*, pp. 39, 47, and 52.

59. Almost two years after his 1977 arrest, the former secretary of agrarian reform, Félix Barra García, was found guilty of extortion and fraud, sentenced to four years in prison, and fined 7.3 million pesos.

According to one report, this was the highest fine for corruption in the history of Mexico. Later, Barra won an appeal and was reportedly freed. See *Excélsior*, September 24, 1977, p. 1, March 21, 1979, p. 1; and *El Universal*, October 2, 1983, p. 7.

60. In April 1978, following a storm of political protest by opposition parties, Cantú Peña and three other officials of the state-owned coffee firm INMECAFE were indicated for bribery, contraband, forgery, fraud, and tax fraud and sentenced to ten years and five months in prison. The U.S. customs agency estimated that the fraud resulted in the illegal entrance of some 157,000 tons of coffee into the United States between December 1976 and March 1977. See *El Día*, April 28, 1978, p. 7; *Excélsior*, July 13, 1978, p. 20; *El Universal*, January 3, 1981, p. 1; and Medina Macías, *Crónica*, p. 69.

61. In January 1989, federal police backed by the army raided the homes of STPRM leaders Joaquín Hernández Galícia (known as La Quina) and Barragán Camachos to find a large cache of weapons. Both men, notoriously corrupt, were charged with illegal possession of arms and tax evasion. See *Latin American Regional Report* RM 89002 (February 16, 1989): 6–7; Guillermo Correa and Salvador Corro, "El gobierno configura sindicatos a su conveniencia e indigna a los trabajadores," *Proceso* 652 (May 1, 1989): 6–13; "La deuda y la crisis no se resuelven fabricando delitos," *Proceso* 656 (May 29, 1989): 6–15.

62. Reports suggesting that President López Portillo was taking millions of dollars out of the country and spending lavishly on real estate in San Diego began to surface as early as October 1982. Soon after he left office, opposition parties pursued the case, even bringing suit against the former president for peculation of funds. Calling the denouncement "counterrevolutionary" (*Heraldo*, February 11, 1983, p. 3), the government eventually exonerated the former president of all wrongdoing. See *Heraldo*, January 21, 1983, p. 1; *Novedades*, January 29, 1983, p. 1E; *Unomasuno*, February 26, 1983, p. 1; Goodsell, "Mexicans Speak Out"; and Anderson "Mexico Makes Its Presidents Millionaires."

63. The May 1977 discovery by the police of the fraudulent sale of documents permitting tax fraud led to a massive investigation of tax evasion on the part of the Treasury Department. The investigation eventually netted several private companies. See *El Día*, June 1, 1977,

p. 2; *El Nacional,* June 3, 1977, p. 15; and *Excélsior,* June 16, 1977, p. 21. In January 1980, the government began an investigation of eight hundred companies (mainly multinational firms) for tax evasion and the illegal withdrawal of money from the country. By March, the attorney general's office confirmed the payment of 450 million pesos by the guilty parties and emphasized that the investigation would continue. See *Excélsior,* January 22, 1980, p. 1; *El Día,* January 24, 1980, p. 1; *Universal,* March 29, 1980, p. 1).

64. This scandal involved a 50-million-peso bribe of a federal judge in the state of Zacatecas, Serrano Robles, in return for the granting of an *amparo* (appeal) to a large landowner in 1980. The case ignited significant political protest and debate centering on the use and misuse of the *amparo,* land fraud in the countryside, and the problems of the peasantry. See *El Día,* July 2, 1980, p. 2; *Excélsior,* July 6, 1980, p. 12; *El Día,* July 5, 1980, p. 2.

65. In February 1989, Eduardo Legorretta Chauvet, the head of Operadora de Bolsa (a large brokerage house), the member of a prominent family (his father was chairman of Banamex Bank), and a personal friend of De la Madrid and Salinas, along with two other officials from Mexicana de Valores e Inversiones, were arrested charged with making short-term loans backed by Cetes that had already matured and doing it right before tax time. See *Latin American Regional Report* RM 89-03 (March 23, 1989): 6; and Carlos Acosta, "Petricioli: Protegió los ilícitos bursátiles, con Anuencia de De la Madrid" *Proceso* 642 (February, 1989): 6–13.

Chapter 4

1. On corruption as an allocative device see Nas, Price, and Weber, "Policy-Oriented Theory"; and Tilman, "Emergence of Black Market Bureaucracy."

2. Huntington, *Political Order,* p. 64; E. L. McKitrick, "The Study of Corruption," *Political Science Quarterly* 72 (1957): 502–14.

3. Purcell and Purcell, "Nature of the Mexican State," p. 13.

4. Knight, *Mexican Revolution,* p. 459.

5. See, for example, the discussion on the Mexican military in Lieuwen, *Arms and Politics,* pp. 101–21.

6. Nye, "Corruption and Political Development."

7. This function of corruption is highlighted by Leff, "Economic Development."

8. Grindle, *Bureaucrats*, p. 75n.

9. *El Sol*, February 24, 1979, p. 1.

10. Scott, *Comparative Political Corruption*, in particular underscores this function of corruption.

11. See, for example, *El Nacional*, September 28, 1983, p. 5; *El Sol*, July 2, 1983, p. 1.

12. Scott, *Comparative Political Corruption*, pp. 20–33.

13. This quote comes from an anonymous reviewer of the journal *Corruption and Reform*.

14. Cornelius, *Politics and the Migrant Poor*, p. 209.

15. Johnson, *Mexican Democracy*, pp. 32 and 116.

16. *Unomasuno*, September 5, 1979, p. 1.

17. *Universal*, May 19, 1982, p. 17.

18. Cited in Riding, *Distant Neighbors*, p. 174.

19. Ibid., p. 175.

20. See Victor T. Le Vine, *Political Corruption: The Ghana Case* (Stanford: Hoover Institution Press, 1975); and Myrdal, "Corruption as a Hindrance."

21. Le Vine, *Political Corruption*, p. 8.

22. Simeha B. Werner, "New Directions in the Study of Administrative Corruption," *Public Administration Review* 43 (1983): 149–50; Tannenbaum, *Mexico*, p. 79; Florescano quoted in Carballo, "Enrique Florescano," pp. 14–15.

23. *Unomasuno*, November 23, 1983, p. 5.

24. Riding, *Distant Neighbors*, p. 178.

25. *El Sol*, May 18, 1976, p. 11.

26. *Excélsior*, January 24, 1983, p. 29.

27. Ibid., August 22, 1980, p. 1.

28. Discussions with a scholar and former member of the Mexican foreign service in Puebla, Mexico, May 19, 1986.

29. See Octavio Paz, *The Labyrinth of Solitude* (New York: Grove Press, 1961).

30. Romanucci-Ross, *Conflict*, p. 121.

31. Werner, "New Directions," pp. 149–50.

32. Quoted in Stockton, "Bribes Are Called a Way of Life."
33. Romanucci-Ross, *Conflict*, p. 117.
34. See Almond and Verba, *Civic Culture*, pp. 112–14; Cornelius, *Politics and the Migrant Poor*; and Davis, "Toward an Explanation."
35. Quoted in Coleman, "Public Opinion," p. 9.
36. Vera, "Capitalismo y corrupción," p. 27.
37. *Unomasuno*, November 6, 1985.
38. *Excélsior*, February 17, 1986, p. 2.
39. *Unomasuno*, November 28, 1978, p. 6.
40. *Información Sistemática*, July 1984, p. 39.
41. *Latin American Regional Report* RM 89-03 (March 23, 1989): 6.
42. *El Heraldo*, October 19, 1976, p. 3.
43. Ibid., June 7, 1977, p. 7.
44. See Gronbeck, "Rhetoric of Political Corruption."
45. Knight, *Mexican Revolution*, p. 503.
46. See Brock, "To the Corrupt Go the Spoils."
47. Alan P. L. Liu, "The Politics of Corruption in the People's Republic of China," *American Political Science Review* 77 (1983): 602–23, provides an empirical examination of this aspect of corruption in the case of China.
48. Quoted in Grindle, *Bureaucrats*, pp. 58–59n.
49. *Excélsior*, March 23, 1978, p. 10.
50. Riding, *Distant Neighbors*, p. 183. Eugenio Méndez Docurro, subsecretary of education under the López Portillo administration, was arrested for peculation and fraud along with four other officials in March 1978. The case ignited great controversy with many expressing support for Méndez. The Popular Socialist party argued that officials with nationalist ideologies were being prosecuted, and the Communist party called it a political vendetta. Méndez also received signs of public support from officials of the Polytechnic Institute (where he had served as director) and Social Security Institute for State Employees (ISSSTE). Eventually, Méndez was sentenced to six months in prison and prohibited from holding public office for two years. See *El Día*, March 23, 1978, p. 6, and April 6, 1978, p. 1; *Excélsior*, March 23, 1978, p. 10, and March 26, 1978, p. 8; and Medina Macías, *Crónica*, p. 56.

The arrest of Cantú Peña of the state coffee firm INMECAFE for fraud in April 1978 triggered a similar series of charges. The Mexican Workers party and Socialist Workers party called the detention part of the government's campaign "against progressive officials." After being indicted for bribery, contraband, forgery, fraud, and tax fraud, Cantú Peña was formally sentenced to 10 years and 5 months in prison, although he won his freedom less than a year later. See *El Día*, April 27, 1978, p. 7, and April 28, 1978, p. 7; *Excélsior*, April 26, 1978, p. 1, July 12, 1978, p. 1, and July 13, 1978, p. 20; *Unomasuno*, April 27, 1978, p. 3; *Universal*, January 3, 1981, p. 1; and Medina Macías, *Crónica*, p. 69.

51. *Mexico City News*, July 1, 1983, p. 12.

52. *El Universal*, October 4, 1977, p. 5.

53. Howard J. Wiarda, "Mexico: The Unraveling of a Corporatist Regime?" *Journal of Interamerican Studies and World Affairs* 30, no. 4 (1988–89): 3.

Chapter 5

1. On the impact of the *sexenio* on Mexican politics see Grindle, *Bureaucrats*; Smith, *Labyrinths of Power*; and Dale Story, "Policy Cycles in Mexican Presidential Politics," *Latin American Research Review* 20 (1985): 139–62.

2. Medina Macías, *Crónica*, p. 78.

3. Oscar Hinojosa, "Investigación y hasta juicio político a De la Madrid: Muñoz Ledo," *Proceso* 659 (June 19, 1989): 19.

4. See *Excélsior*, January 6, 1978, p. 21; and Medina Macías, *Crónica*, p. 37.

5. *Excélsior*, January 29, 1976, p. 1; *El Día*, February 4, 1976, p. 1, and February 7, 1976, p. 1, June 25, 1976, p. 1, January 16, 1977, p. 3; and *Excélsior*, January 23, 1977, p. 24.

6. *Universal*, October 1, 1981, p. 1.

7. Secretaría de Gobernación, *Renovación moral de la sociedad* (México: Talleres Gráficos de la Nación, 1983), p. 22.

8. *Ovaciones*, October 5, 1977, p. 1; *El Sol*, February 28, 1977, p. 2; *El Heraldo*, October 12, 1977, p. 1; *La Prensa*, December 8, 1980, p. 3; *El Día*, April 16, 1978, p. 1; *Excélsior*, April 17, 1978, p. 1; and *Unomasuno*, March 17, 1980, p. 27.

9. *Excélsior,* June 19, 1977, p. 1.

10. Judith Adler Hellman, *Mexico in Crisis* (New York: Holmes and Meier, 1978), p. 150; *El Día,* June 25, 1976, p. 1.

11. *Novedades,* December 6, 1983, p. 1.

12. *La Prensa,* June 24, 1977, p. 9.

13. See, for example, *El Heraldo,* September 25, 1977, p. 7; and *Universal,* September 27, 1977, p. 1.

14. *El Día,* May 10, 1978, p. 2; and *Universal,* May 22, 1978, p. 1.

15. *Unomasuno,* February 10, 1980, p. 27.

16. *Universal,* October 24, 1983, p. 1.

17. *Información Sistemática,* September 1984, p. 35.

18. Stockton, "Bribes Are Called a Way of Life"; Larry Rohter, "Mexico Taking Bites out of Corruption," *Arizona Daily Star,* April 19, 1987, p. 7; *Mexico Today,* October 1986, p. 7.

19. On investigations and prosecutions in various bureaucratic agencies see *El Día,* March 25, 1977, p. 8; *El Sol,* March 8, 1977, p. 10, March 22, 1977, p. 12; and *Excélsior,* March 4, 1977, p. 23, March 10, 1977, p. 6, and March 29, 1977, p. 27.

20. *El Sol,* January 4, 1977, p. 1; *El Día,* January 8, 1977, p. 17; *Unomasuno,* September 8, 1979, p. 1.

21. *Excélsior,* February 19, 1977, p. 1; *Unomasuno,* November 8, 1978, p. 1.

22. *Excélsior,* June 20, 1977, p. 7.

23. *Unomasuno,* November 1, 1978, p. 3, and November 7, 1979, p. 1.

24. *Universal,* November 16, 1979, p. 1.

25. Medina Macías, *Crónica,* p. 42.

26. On these reforms see María del Carmen Prado, "La reforma administrativa para el desarrollo social en México," *Foro Internacional* 25, no. 2 (1984): 101–17.

27. *Tiempo* 73 (July 1978): 7.

28. *Excélsior,* October 24, 1979, p. 4.

29. On this anticorruption campaign see Secretaría de Gobernación, *Renovación Moral;* Presidencia de la República, Unidad de la Crónica Presidencial, *Las razones y las obras: Gobierno de Miguel de la Madrid,* 2 vols. (México: Presidencia de la República, 1984, 1985).

30. In a private conversation, an attorney within the Comptroller's

office predicted that the agency would not survive for more than one or two *sexenios* and that many in the government considered the agency a mere political ploy.

31. See *Excélsior,* May 29, 1983, p. 4, and July 1, 1983, p. 18.

32. *El Sol,* January 14, 1983, p. 1.

33. On this program see Presidencia de la República, *Razones,* pp. 528–30.

34. *Novedades,* December 6, 1983, p. 1.

35. Cindy Anders, "Five Years Later . . . One Answer, Countless Questions," *Mexico Journal* 2, no. 35 (June 26, 1989): 22.

36. See *El Heraldo,* November 22, 1977, p. 11; and *Novedades,* November 24, 1977, p. 1.

37. See *Excélsior,* February 17, 1983, p. 4; *El Heraldo,* February 11, 1983, p. 3; and *Unomasuno,* February 26, 1983, p. 1.

38. Hellman, *Mexico in Crisis,* p. 150.

39. *El Heraldo,* April 28, 1978, p. 2.

40. It is perhaps incredible that even officials supposedly deeply involved in attacking corruption such as Echeverría and López Portillo were later either found culpable or strongly suspected of corruption. The police chief Durazo, for instance, prided himself on his anticorruption position. In other examples, Díaz Serrano declared in 1976 that PEMEX was clean of corrupt networks (*El Día,* December 31, 1976, p. 7); Hank González (mayor of Mexico City, who later was said to have acquired a fortune from the illegal sale of *ejido* or communal lands) attacked land fraud (*El Día,* December 15, 1976, p. 21); and Hernández Galícia (prominent petroleum labor leader suspected of illicit fortunes) called for the eradication of corruption in the petroleum industry (*Excélsior,* October 13, 1977, p. 12). Equally incredible, perhaps, one agent of the Public Ministry provided the reassuring calculation that corruption would be eliminated in 20 *sexenios* (120 years) (*Excélsior,* June 6, 1980, p. 4).

41. Sanders, *Mexico,* p. 71; Brinkley, "Mexico and the Narcotics Traffic," p. 4.

42. Brock, "To the Corrupt Go the Spoils."

43. See *Mexico Journal* 1, no. 34 (1988): 11; and "Interview with Jorge Obrador Capellini," *Mexico Journal* 1, no. 36 (1988): 4.

44. See Anders, "Five Years Later"; Enrique Maza, "La Renovación

Moral, seis años de incubación o Solapamiento de delincuentes," *Proceso* 659 (June 19, 1989): 20–21; Leon Lazaroff, "The Official Story," *Mexico Journal*, July 10, 1989, p. 6.

45. *Proceso* 659 (June 19, 1989): 18.

46. See Maza, "Renovación Moral"; and Acosta, "Petricioli."

47. *Proceso* 659 (June 19, 1989): 19; see also Maza, "Renovación Moral."

48. *Mexico Journal*, 2, no. 35 (June 26, 1989): 14.

49. Joe Kennan, "A Common Crook's behind Bars Today," *Mexico Journal*, 2, no. 35 (June 26, 1989): 3.

50. Anders, "Five Years Later," p. 22.

51. *Mexico Journal* 2, no. 37 (July 10, 1989): 10; and Cristina Montaño and Daniel M. Lund, "Erosion of PRI Support and Credibility: *Los Angeles Times* Mexico Poll," *Interamerican Public Opinion Report*, January 1990, p. 3.

52. *Latin America Weekly Report* 89-22 (June 8, 1989): 10.

53. *Proceso* 659 (June 19, 1989): 18.

Chapter 6

1. Earlier public opinion surveys in Mexico have focused on political culture, support for democracy and for the system, government performance, and the economic crisis; none has focused directly on attitudes related to political corruption. See Almond and Verba, *Civic Culture*; Booth and Seligson, "Political Culture"; Davis, "Toward an Explanation"; and "New York Times Poll, Mexican Survey," October 28–November 4, 1986.

2. The appendix describes the methods followed in the survey and provides a copy and translation of the questionnaire.

3. Gamma and tau measure degree of association among nominal and ordinal values.

4. *Mexico Journal* 2, no. 37 (July 10, 1989): 10; see also Montaño and Lund, "Erosion of PRI Support."

5. Edward N. Muller, Thomas O. Jukam, and Mitchell A. Seligson "Diffuse Political Support and Antisystem Political Behavior: A Comparative Analysis," *American Journal of Political Science* 26 (1982):

240–64, show support for the ruling party to be an important indicator of diffuse support for the system.

6. See data from Booth and Seligson, "Political Culture."

Chapter 7

1. Wiarda, "Mexico," p. 4.

2. On various aspects of the crises see Roderic Ai Camp, ed., *Mexico's Political Stability: The Next Five Years* (Boulder, Colo.: Westview Press, 1986); Wayne A. Cornelius, Judith Gentleman, and Peter H. Smith, eds., *Mexico's Alternative Political Futures*, Monograph Series 30 (San Diego: Center for U.S.-Mexican Studies, University of California, 1989); Judith Gentleman, ed., *Mexican Politics in Transition*, Westview Special Studies on Latin America and the Caribbean (Boulder, Colo.: Westview Press, 1987); Judith Gentleman, "Prospects for Stability and Change in Mexico," *Latin American Research Review* 23, no. 3 (1988): 188–98; Brian Latell, *Mexico at the Crossroads: The Many Crises of the Political System* (Stanford: Hoover Institute Press, 1986); Daniel Levy, "The Mexican Government's Loosening Grip?" *Current History*, March 1987, pp. 113–16, 132–33; James H. Street, "Mexico's Development Crisis," *Current History*, March 1987, pp. 101–4 and 127–29; Donald L. Wyman, *Mexico's Economic Crisis: Challenges and Opportunities*, Monograph Series, 12 (San Diego: Center for U.S.-Mexican Studies, University of California, 1983).

3. Kevin J. Middlebrook, "The Sounds of Silence: Organized Labour's Response to Economic Crisis in Mexico," *Journal of Latin American Studies* 21, no. 2 (1989): 195; see also Jeffrey Bortz, "The Dilemma of Mexican Labor," *Current History*, March 1987, p. 107.

4. Montaño and Lund, "Erosion of PRI Support."

5. See Lawrence Rout, "Mexicans, in Depths of Crisis, Are Irked by Allegations Leaders Spend Lavishly," *Wall Street Journal*, September 20, 1982, p. 28.

6. *El Heraldo*, July 10, 1983, p. 1.

7. *Excélsior*, April 8, 1983, p. 5; *Información Sistemática*, May 1984, p. 41.

8. *Mexico City News*, December 4, 1985.

9. This idea was elaborated in an interview with a leftist activist and journalist in Mexico City.

10. *Universal*, August 3, 1982, p. 12; *Información Sistemática*, February 1983, Ref #4030.

11. *El Heraldo*, May 17, 1982, p. 1. On a theoretical level, others have discussed corruption as a factor contributing to revolution and military coup. See, for example, discussion on Aaron's views on corruption in Willem F. Wertheim, "Sociological Aspects of Corruption in Southeast Asia," *Sociologica Neerlandica* 1, no. 2. (Autumn 1963): 129–52, rpt. in Heidenheimer, ed., *Political Corruption*, p. 195; Myrdal, "Corruption as a Hindrance," p. 229.

12. Brock, "To the Corrupt Go the Spoils."

13. See *Unomasuno*, January 27, 1983, p. 4.

14. *El Heraldo*, May 2, 1983, p. 2; and *Novedades*, May 20, 1983, p. 10.

15. See Rosenblaum, "Wall of Corruption."

16. See Rout, "Mexicans," p. 28.

17. Huntington, *Political Order*, p. 61.

18. Quoted in Brinkley, "Mexico and the Narcotics Traffic."

19. Riding, *Distant Neighbors*, pp. 167–68.

20. On corruption related to the growth of oil revenues see George Grayson, *The Politics of Mexican Oil* (Pittsburgh: University of Pittsburgh Press, 1981); Ramírez, "Finanzas de PEMEX"; and Flavio Tavares, "The Shame of Mexico: Corruption and Mismanagement in a Sea of Oil," *World Press Report* 30 (1983): 26–28.

21. Johnston, "Political Consequences of Corruption," p. 473.

22. Riding, *Distant Neighbors*, pp. 167–68.

23. See Brinkley, "Mexico and the Narcotics Traffic"; and John J. Fialka, "Death of US Agent in Mexico Drug Case Uncovers Grid of Graft," *Wall Street Journal*, November 19, 1986, pp. 1, 20.

24. *Excélsior*, November 5, 1980, p. 4.

25. See, for example, *Unomasuno*, October 18, 1985, p. 1, and November 7, 1985, p. 1.

26. On privatization see Bela Balassa, Gerardo M. Bueno, Pedro-Pablo Kuczynski, and Mario Henrique Simonsen, *Toward Renewed Economic Growth in Latin America* (Washington, D.C.: Institute for International Economics, 1987), p. 144; Larry Rohter, "Shedding the

Losers," *Arizona Daily Star,* April 19, 1987, p. 5; and Schneider, "Partly for Sale."

27. *Latin American Weekly Report* 89-21 (June 1, 1989): 3.

28. Inter-American Development Bank, *Economic and Social Progress in Latin America* (Washington, D.C.: Inter-American Development Bank, 1987), p. 26.

29. Schneider, "Partly for Sale," p. 102.

30. Bortz, "Dilemma of Mexican Labor," p. 127.

31. On the new business environment see Rubin, *Mexico.*

32. Allison Perey, "The Revolutionary Potential of Mexico in the 1980s," *Journal of International Affairs* 40, no. 2 (1987): 373–85; also see Leopoldo Gómez and Joseph L. Klesner, "Mexico's 1988 Elections: The Beginning of a New Era in Mexican Politics?" *LASA Forum* 19, no. 3. (1989): 1, 3–8.

33. See *Mexico Today,* November 1986, pp. 2–4; for an overview and analysis of political reform see Gentleman, ed., *Mexican Politics.*

34. Steven E. Sanderson, "Presidential Succession and Political Rationality in Mexico," *World Politics* 35 (1983): 323.

35. John Bailey, "The Impact of Major Groups on Policy-Making Trends in Government-Business Relations in Mexico," in Camp, ed., *Mexico's Political Stability,* pp. 119–42; and Peter H. Smith, "Leadership and Change: Intellectuals and Technocrats in Mexico," ibid., 104–9.

36. Levy, "Political Consequences."

37. See Kevin J. Middlebrook, "Dilemmas of Change in Mexican Politics," *World Politics* 41, no. 1 (1988): 120–41; and Middlebrook, "Sounds of Silence."

38. See Bortz, "Dilemma of Mexican Labor," p. 108.

39. Guillermo Correa and Salvador Corro, "En sus nuevas relaciones con el sindicalismo oficial, al gobierno ya no le sirve Fidel," *Proceso* 641 (February 13, 1989): 6–9.

40. *Latin American Weekly Report* 89-35 (September 7, 1989): 8; and Schneider, "Partly for Sale," p. 104.

41. See Sanderson, "Presidential Succession," p. 321.

42. Cox, "Changes in the Mexican Political System," pp. 20, 22; Camp, *Mexico's Political Stability,* p. 3.

43. Wilkie, "Dramatic Growth," p. 39, suggests that this is also true for the president.

44. Brock, "To the Corrupt Go the Spoils."
45. See *El Día*, August 1, 1980, p. 1; and *Excélsior*, August 21, 1980, p. 1.
46. *Novedades*, January 29, 1983, p. 3E; *El Heraldo*, January 21, 1983, p. 1, March 31, 1983, p. 12, and April 24, 1983, p. 2.
47. *Mexico City News*, October 22, 1985.
48. *Latin American Weekly Report* 89-3 (September 21, 1989): 8.
49. *Unomasuno*, December 5, 1981, p. 32; *Mexico City News*, October 22, 1985.
50. See interview with Eduardo Valle, *Mexico Journal* 2, no. 35 (June 26, 1989): 19–20.
51. Smith, "Leadership and Change," p. 106.
52. Middlebrook, "Dilemmas," p. 134.
53. Ibid., p. 127.
54. Middlebrook, "Sounds of Silence," p. 219.
55. Sixteen candidates from labor were defeated in the 1988 elections. See Correa and Corro, "En sus nuevas relaciones," p. 8.
56. Cornelius, Gentleman, and Smith, eds., *Mexico's Alternative Political Futures*, p. 33.
57. Ibid., pp. 25, 19, 22.
58. Salvador Castañeda S., "Llama Salinas a los priístas a trabajar para merecer el voto," *Novedades*, December 14, 1989, p. 18.
59. Editorial in *La Voz de Michoacán*, quoted in Cindy Anders, "Premodern Politics," *Mexico Journal*, July 24, 1989, p. 7.
60. *Latin American Weekly Report* 89-30 (August 3, 1989): 10.
61. "Las principales críticas de Luis J. Garrido en gobernación, a gobernación," *Proceso* 642 (February 20, 1989): 30–31.
62. See Kenneth M. Coleman and Charles L. Davis, "Preemptive Reform and the Mexican Working Class," *Latin American Research Review* 18, no. 1 (1983): 3–32; Perey, "Revolutionary Potential," p. 380.

Conclusion

1. Etzioni, *Capital Corruption*, p. 269.
2. Huntington, *Political Order*, p. 61; Johnson, *Mexican Democracy*, p. 33.

Appendix

1. This question and the following one were taken from Arthur H. Miller, "Political Issues and Trust in Government," *American Political Science Review* 68 (1974): 951–72.

Bibliography

Articles and Books

Abueva, José Velasco. "The Contribution of Nepotism, Spoils and Graft to Political Development." *East-West Center Review* 3 (1966): 45–54.

Acosta, Carlos. "Petricioli: Protegió los ilícitos bursátiles, con anuencia de De la Madrid." *Proceso* 642 (February 20, 1989): 6–13.

Acosta Romero, Miguel. "Mexican Federalism: Conception and Reality." *Public Administration Review* 42, no. 5 (1982): 399–404.

Adie, Robert F. "Cooperation, Cooptation and Conflict in Mexican Peasant Organizations." *Interamerican Economic Affairs* 24, no. 3 (1970): 3–25.

Almond, Gabriel, and Sidney Verba. *The Civic Culture: Political Attitudes and Democracy in Five Nations.* Princeton: Princeton University Press, 1963.

Anders, Cindy. "Five Years Later . . . One Answer, Countless Questions." *Mexico Journal* 2, no. 35 (June 26, 1989): 16–22.

———. "Premodern Politics." *Mexico Journal,* July 24, 1989, p. 7.

Anderson, Bo, and James Cockcroft. "Control and Cooptation in Mexican Politics." *International Journal of Comparative Sociology* 7 (1966): 11–28.

Anderson, Jack. "Mexican Wheels Are Lubricated by Official Oil." *Washington Post,* May 14, 1984, p. 11B.

———. "Mexico Makes Its Presidents Millionaires." *Washington Post*, May 15, 1984, p. 15C.

Andreski, Stanislav. "Kleptocracy or Corruption as a System of Government." In *The African Predicament*, pp. 92–109. New York: Atherton, 1968. Reprinted as "Kleptocracy as a System of Government in Africa." In *Political Corruption: Readings in Comparative Analysis*, edited by Arnold J. Heidenheimer, pp. 346–60. New York: Holt, Rinehart and Winston, 1970.

Bailey, John. "The Impact of Major Groups on Policy-Making Trends in Government-Business Relations in Mexico." In *Mexico's Political Stability: The Next Five Years*, edited by Roderic Ai Camp, pp. 119–42. Boulder, Colo.: Westview Press, 1986.

Balassa, Bela, Gerardo M. Bueno, Pedro-Pablo Kuczynski, and Mario Henrique Simonsen. *Toward Renewed Economic Growth in Latin America*. Washington, D.C.: Institute for International Economics, 1987.

Ballard, Perry. "El modelo liberal y la política práctica." *Historia Mexicana* 23, no. 4 (1974): 646–99.

Banfield, Edward C. *The Moral Basis of a Backward Society*. New York: Free Press, 1958.

Bayley, David H. "The Effects of Corruption in a Developing Country." *Western Political Quarterly* 19 (1966): 719–32. Reprinted in *Political Corruption: Readings in Comparative Analysis*, edited by Arnold J. Heidenheimer, pp. 521–33. New York: Holt, Rinehart and Winston, 1970.

Ben-Dor, Gabriel. "Corruption, Institutionalization, and Political Development: The Revisionist Theses Revisited." *Comparative Political Studies* 7 (1974): 63–83.

Benson, George. *Political Corruption in America*. Lexington, Mass.: Lexington Books, 1978.

Biles, Robert E. "The Position of the Judiciary in the Political Systems of Argentina and Mexico." *Lawyer of the Americas* 8, no. 2 (1980): 287–318.

Booth, John A., and Mitchell A. Seligson. "The Political Culture of Authoritarianism in Mexico: A Re-Examination." *Latin American Research Review* 19, no. 1 (1984): 106–24.

Bortz, Jeffrey. "The Dilemma of Mexican Labor." *Current History*, March 1987, pp. 105–8, 129–30.

Brading, David A. "El estado en México en la época de los Habsburgos." *Historia Mexicana* 23, no. 4 (1974): 551–610.

Brandenburg, Frank. *The Making of Modern Mexico.* Englewood Cliffs, N.J.: Prentice-Hall, 1964.

Brasz, H. A. "Some Notes on the Sociology of Corruption." *Sociologica Neerlandica* (Autumn 1963): 111–17, 117–25. Reprinted as "The Sociology of Corruption" and "Administrative Corruption in Theory and Dutch Practice." In *Political Corruption: Readings and Comparative Analysis*, edited by Arnold J. Heidenheimer, pp. 41–45 and 243–48. New York: Holt, Rinehart and Winston, 1970.

Brinkley, Joel. "Mexico and the Narcotics Traffic: Growing Strain in US Relations." *New York Times*, October 20, 1986, p. 4.

Brock, David. "To the Corrupt Go the Spoils for More Than Half a Century." *Insight*, October 5, 1987, p. 1.

Cabildo, Miguel. "Durazo obligaba a su personal al entregarle el producto de sus mordidas." *Proceso* 386 (May 26, 1984): 16–17.

Camp, Roderic Ai. *The Making of a Government: Political Leaders in Modern Mexico.* Tucson: University of Arizona Press, 1984.

———. *Mexico's Political Stability: The Next Five Years.* Boulder, Colo.: Westview Press, 1986.

Carballo, Marco Aurelio. "Enrique Florescano: La corrupción forma de control político." *Proceso* 39 (August 1, 1977): 14–15.

Carpizo, Jorge. "The No Re-election Principle in Mexico." *Mexican Forum* 3, no. 4 (1983): 9–13.

Castañeda S., Salvador. "Llama Salinas a los priístas a trabajar para merecer el voto." *Novedades*, December 14, 1989, p. 18.

Castilla, Armando. *El caso de Flores Tápia.* México: Grijalbo, 1982.

Cepeda, Miguel. "En 13 años, Flores Tápia pasó de la quiebra a la riqueza." *Proceso* 240 (June 6, 1981): 21–24.

Chávez, Elías. "La Ley de Responsibilidades, violatoria de la Constitución." *Proceso* 238 (May 25, 1981): 12–13.

Cockcroft, James. "Coercion and Ideology in Mexican Politics." In *Dependence and Underdevelopment: Latin America's Political Economy*, edited by James Cockcroft et al. Garden City, N.Y.: Doubleday Anchor Press, 1972.

Coleman, Kenneth M. *Public Opinion in Mexico City about the Elec-*

toral System. James Sprunt Series in History and Political Science, no. 53. Chapel Hill: University of North Carolina Press, 1972.

Coleman, Kenneth M., and Charles L. Davis. "Preemptive Reform and the Mexican Working Class." *Latin American Research Review* 18, no. 1 (1983): 3–32.

Cornelius, Wayne A. *Politics and the Migrant Poor in Mexico City.* Stanford: Stanford University Press, 1975.

Cornelius, Wayne A., Judith Gentleman, and Peter H. Smith, eds. *Mexico's Alternative Political Futures.* Monograph Series 30. San Diego: Center for U.S.-Mexican Studies, University of California, 1989.

Correa, Guillermo, and Salvador Corro. "El gobierno configura sindicatos a su conveniencia e indigna a los trabajadores." *Proceso* 652 (May 1, 1989): 6–13.

———. "En sus nuevas relaciones con el sindicalismo oficial, al gobierno ya no le sirve Fidel." *Proceso* 641 (February 13, 1989): 6–9.

Corro, Salvador. "Ofensiva final en Ciudad Madero, para acabar con todo vestigio quinista." *Proceso* 658 (June 12, 1989): 10–15.

Cox, Norman. "Changes in the Mexican Political System." In *Politics in Mexico,* edited by George Philip, pp. 15–53. London: Croom Helm, 1985.

Davis, Charles L. "Toward an Explanation of Mass Support for Authoritarian Regimes: A Case Study of Political Attitudes in Mexico City." Ph.D. dissertation, University of Kentucky, 1974.

de la Peña, Guillermo. *A Legacy of Promises: Agriculture, Politics and Ritual in the Morelos Highlands of Mexico.* Austin: University of Texas Press, 1981.

del Carmen Prado, María. "La reforma administrativa para el desarrollo social en México." *Foro Internacional* 25, no. 2 (1984): 101–17.

Deysine, Anne. "Political Corruption: A Review of the Literature." *European Journal of Political Research* 8 (1980): 447–62.

Dowse, Robert. "Conceptualizing Corruption." Review of *Society and Bureaucracy in Contemporary Ghana* by Robert M. Price. *Government and Opposition* 12 (1977): 244–54.

Eckstein, Susan. *The Poverty of Revolution.* Princeton: Princeton University Press, 1977.

Edelman, Murray. *The Symbolic Uses of Politics*. Champaign-Urbana: University of Illinois Press, 1964.

Etzioni, Amitai. *Capital Corruption: The New Attack on American Democracy*. San Diego: Harcourt, 1984.

Fagen, Richard R., and William S. Tuohy. *Politics and Privilege in a Mexican City*. Stanford: Stanford University Press, 1972.

Fialka, John J. "Death of US Agent in Mexico Drug Case Uncovers Grid of Graft." *Wall Street Journal*, November 19, 1986, pp. 1, 20.

Friedrich, Carl J. *The Pathology of Politics: Violence, Betrayal, Corruption, Secrecy and Propaganda*. New York: Harper & Row, 1972.

Galarza, Gerardo. "Biebrich recupera algo lo que le arrebató el celo por sus éxitos." *Proceso* 386 (March 26, 1984): 13–15.

Gentleman, Judith. "Prospects for Stability and Change in Mexico." *Latin American Research Review* 23, no. 3 (1988): 188–98.

————, ed. *Mexican Politics in Transition*. Westview Special Studies on Latin America and the Caribbean. Boulder, Colo.: Westview Press, 1987.

Glade, William P., Jr., and Charles W. Anderson. *The Political Economy of Mexico*. Madison: University of Wisconsin Press, 1963.

Gómez, Leopoldo, and Joseph L. Klesner. "Mexico's 1988 Elections: The Beginning of a New Era in Mexican Politics?" *LASA Forum* 19, no. 3 (1989): 1, 3–8.

González Casanova, Pablo. *La democracia en México*. 14th ed. México: Era, 1965.

González González, José. *Lo negro del negro Durazo*. México: Posada, 1983.

Goodsell, James Nelson. "Mexicans Speak out against Government Corruption." *Christian Science Monitor*, October 6, 1982, pp. 1, 6.

Graham, Lawrence S. *Politics in a Mexican Community*. Latin American Monograph Series 1, no. 35. Gainesville: University of Florida Press, 1968.

Grayson, George. *The Politics of Mexican Oil*. Pittsburgh: University of Pittsburgh Press, 1981.

Greenberg, Martin. *Bureaucracy and Development: A Mexican Case Study*. Lexington, Mass: Heath Lexington, 1970.

Grindle, Merilee Serrill. *Bureaucrats, Politicians and Peasants in Mexico: A Case Study in Public Policy*. Berkeley and Los Angeles: University of California Press, 1977.

Gronbeck, Bruce E. "The Rhetoric of Political Corruption: Socio-linguistic, Dialectical and Ceremonial Processes." *Quarterly Journal of Speech* 64 (1984): 155–72.

Hansen, Roger D. *The Politics of Mexican Development.* Baltimore: Johns Hopkins Press, 1971.

Hanson, Mark. "Organizational Bureaucracy in Latin America and the Legacy of Spanish Colonialism." *Journal of Interamerican Studies and World Affairs* 16, no. 2 (1974): 199–219.

Heidenheimer, Arnold J., ed. *Political Corruption: Readings in Comparative Analysis.* New York: Holt, Rinehart and Winston, 1970.

Hellman, Judith Adler. *Mexico in Crisis.* New York: Holmes and Meier, 1978.

Hinojosa, Oscar. "Investigación y hasta juicio político a De la Madrid: Muñoz Ledo." *Proceso* 659 (June 19, 1989): 19.

Holloway, Harry, and Frank S. Meyers. "Refining the Definition of Corruption: Reflections from an Oklahoma Study." Paper presented at the Southwestern Political Science Association meeting, Houston, Texas, March 20–23, 1985.

Hoselitz, Bert F. "Levels of Economic Performance and Bureaucratic Structures." In *Bureaucracy and Political Development,* edited by Joseph La Palombara, pp. 188–96. Princeton: Princeton University Press, 1963. Reprinted as "Performance Levels and Bureaucratic Structure." In *Political Corruption: Readings and Comparative Analysis,* edited by Arnold J. Heidenheimer, pp. 76–81. New York: Holt, Rinehart and Winston, 1970.

Huntington, Samuel P. *Political Order in Changing Societies.* New Haven: Yale University Press, 1968.

Inter-American Development Bank. *Economic and Social Progress in Latin America.* Washington, D.C.: Inter-American Development Bank, 1987.

"Interview with Jorge Obrador Capellini." *Mexico Journal* 1, no. 36 (1988): 4.

Johnson, Kenneth F. *Mexican Democracy: A Critical View.* Rev. ed. New York: Praeger, 1984.

———. "The 1980 Image-Index Survey of Latin American Political Democracy." *Latin American Research Review* 17, no. 3 (1982): 193–201.

Johnson, Omotunde E. G. "An Economic Analysis of Corrupt Government with Special Application to Less Developed Countries." *Kylos* 28 (1975): 47–61.

Johnston, Michael. "The Political Consequences of Corruption: A Reassessment." *Comparative Politics* 18, no. 4 (1986): 459–77.

Kautsky, John. *Patterns of Modernizing Revolutions: Mexico and the Soviet Union.* Sage Professional Papers in Comparative Politics, Vol. 5, Ser. 01-156. Beverly Hills: Sage, 1975.

Kelley, Guillermo. "Politics and Administration in Mexico: Recruitment and Promotion of the Politico-Administrative Class." *Mexican Forum* 1, no. 4 (1981): 8–11.

Kennan, Joe. "A Common Crook's behind Bars Today." *Mexico Journal* 2, no. 35 (June 26, 1989): 3.

Key, V. O., Jr. *Techniques of Political Graft in the United States,* pp. 386–401. Chicago: University of Chicago Libraries, 1936. Reprinted as "Techniques of Political Graft." In *Political Corruption: Readings and Comparative Analysis,* edited by Arnold J. Heidenheimer, pp. 46–53. New York: Holt, Rinehart and Winston, 1970.

Kling, Merle. "Towards a Theory of Power and Political Instability in Latin America." *Western Political Science Quarterly* 9, no. 1 (1956): 21–35.

Knight, Alan. *The Mexican Revolution.* Vol 2: *Counter-Revolution and Reconstruction.* New York: Cambridge University Press, 1986.

Koslow, Lawrence E., and Stephen P. Mumme. "The Evolution of the Mexican Political System: A Paradigmatic Analysis." In *The Future of Mexico,* edited by Lawrence E. Koslow, pp. 47–98. Tempe: Arizona State University Center for Latin American Studies, 1981.

"La deuda y la crisis no se resuelven fabricando delitos." *Proceso* 656 (May 29, 1989): 6–15.

"Las principales críticas de Luis J. Garrido en Gobernación, a Gobernación." *Proceso* 642 (February 20, 1989): 30–31.

Latell, Brian. *Mexico at the Crossroads: The Many Crises of the Political System.* Stanford: Hoover Institution Press, 1986.

Lazaroff, Leon. "Adiós DI or Is It Only hasta luego?" *Mexico Journal,* July 10, 1989, p. 7.

———. "The Official Story." *Mexico Journal,* July 10, 1989, p. 6.

Leff, Nathaniel H. "Economic Development through Bureaucratic

Corruption." *American Behavioral Scientist* 8, no. 3 (1964): 8–14. Reprinted in *Political Corruption: Readings and Comparative Analysis*, edited by Arnold J. Heidenheimer, pp. 510–20. New York: Holt, Rinehart and Winston, 1970.

Lemarchand, Rene. "Comparative Political Clientelism: Structure, Process and Optic." In *Political Clientelism, Patronage and Development*, edited by S. N. Eisenstadt and Rene Lemarchand. Beverly Hills: Sage, 1981.

Le Vine, Victor T. *Political Corruption: The Ghana Case*. Stanford: Hoover Institution Press, 1975.

Levy, Daniel. "The Mexican Government's Loosening Grip?" *Current History*, March 1987, pp. 113–16, 132–33.

———. "The Political Consequences of Changing Socialization Patterns." In *Mexico's Political Stability: The Next Five Years*, edited by Roderic Ai Camp, pp. 19–46. Boulder, Colo.: Westview Press, 1986.

———. "University Autonomy in Mexico: Implications for Regime Authoritarianism." *Latin American Research Review* 14, no. 3 (1979): 129–52.

Levy, Daniel, and Gabriel Szekeley. *Mexico: Paradoxes of Stability and Change*. Boulder, Colo.: Westview Press, 1983.

Lewis, Paul H. "Development Strategies and the Decline of the Democratic Left in Latin America." In *The Continuing Struggle for Democracy in Latin America*, edited by Howard J. Wiarda, pp. 185–200. Boulder, Colo.: Westview Press, 1980.

Lieuwen, Edwin. *Arms and Politics in Latin America*. New York: Praeger, 1960.

Liu, Alan P. L. "The Politics of Corruption in the People's Republic of China." *American Political Science Review* 77 (1983): 602–23.

Lomnitz, Claudio. "Compliance and Coalitions in the Mexican Government, 1917–1940." In *Five Centuries of Law and Politics in Central Mexico*, edited by Ronald Spores and Ross Hassig, pp. 173–208. Vanderbilt University Publication in Anthropology 30. Nashville: Vanderbilt University, 1984.

Maza, Enrique. "La Renovación Moral, seis años de incubación o solapamiento de delincuentes." *Proceso* 659 (June 19, 1989): 20–21.

McKitrick, E. L. "The Study of Corruption." *Political Science Quarterly* 72 (1957): 502–14.

McMullan, M. "A Theory of Corruption." *Sociological Review* 9, no. 2 (1961): 181–201.

Medina Macías, Ricardo. *Crónica del desengaño: Cátalogo de la corrupción*. México: Editorial Asociados, 1983.

Meyer, Lorenzo. "Historical Roots of the Authoritarian State in Mexico." In *Authoritarianism in Mexico*, edited by José Luis Reyna and Richard S. Weinert, pp. 3–22. Philadelphia: Institute for the Study of Human Issues, 1977.

Middlebrook, Kevin J. "Dilemmas of Change in Mexican Politics." *World Politics* 41, no. 1 (1988): 120–41.

———. "The Sounds of Silence: Organized Labour's Response to Economic Crisis in Mexico." *Journal of Latin American Studies* 21, no. 2 (1989): 195–220.

Migdal, Joel S. "A Model of State-Society Relations." In *New Directions in Comparative Politics*, edited by Howard J. Wiarda, pp. 41–55. Boulder, Colo.: Westview Press, 1985.

Miller, Arthur H. "Political Issues and Trust in Government." *American Political Science Review* 68 (1974): 951–72.

Montaño, Cristina, and Daniel M. Lund. "Erosion of PRI Support and Credibility: *Los Angeles Times* Mexico Poll." *Interamerican Public Opinion Report*, January 1990, p. 3.

Moodie, Graeme C. "On Political Scandals and Corruption." *Government and Opposition* 15 (1980): 208–22.

Morris, Stephen D. "Corruption and the Mexican Political System." *Corruption and Reform* 2, no. 1 (1987): 3–15.

Mosca, Gaetano. *The Ruling Class*. New York: McGraw-Hill, 1939.

Muller, Edward N., Thomas O. Jukam, and Mitchell A. Seligson. "Diffuse Political Support and Antisystem Political Behavior: A Comparative Analysis." *American Journal of Political Science* 26 (1982): 240–64.

Murray, William K. "Prospects for the Moral Renovation Campaign." Unpublished paper. Glendale, Ariz.: American Graduate School of International Management, 1984.

Myrdal, Gunnar. *Asian Drama: An Enquiry into the Poverty of Nations*, Vol. 2. New York: Twentieth Century Fund, 1968.

———. "Corruption: Its Causes and Effects." In *Asian Drama: An Enquiry into the Poverty of Nations*, 2: 937–58. New York: Twentieth Century Fund, 1968. Reprinted as "Corruption as a Hindrance to Modernization in South Asia" and "Corruption: Its Causes and Effects." In *Political Corruption: Readings and Comparative Analysis*, edited by Arnold J. Heidenheimer, pp. 229–39 and 540–45. New York: Holt, Rinehart and Winston, 1970.

Nagle, John D. *Introduction to Comparative Politics: Political System Performance in Three Worlds*. Chicago: Nelson-Hall, 1989.

Nas, Tevfik F., Albert C. Price, and Charles T. Weber. "A Policy-Oriented Theory of Corruption." *American Political Science Review* 80 (1986): 107–19.

Needleman, Carolyn, and Martin Needleman. "Who Rules Mexico? A Critique of Some Current Views of the Mexican Political Process." *Journal of Politics* 31, no. 4 (1969): 1011–34.

Needler, Martin C. *Politics and Society in Mexico*. Albuquerque: University of New Mexico Press, 1971.

———. "Problems in the Evaluation of the Mexican Political System." In *Contemporary Mexico: Papers of the IV International Congress of Mexican History*, edited by James W. Wilkie, Michael C. Meyer, and Edna Monzon de Wilkie, pp. 339–47. Berkeley and Los Angeles: University of California Press, 1976.

———, ed. *Political Systems of Latin America*. 2d ed. New York: Van Nostrand Reinhold, 1970.

"New York Times Poll, Mexican Survey." October 28–November 4, 1986.

Nye, Joseph S. "Corruption and Political Development: A Cost-Benefit Analysis." *American Political Science Review* 61 (1967): 417–27.

Oszlak, Oscar. "The Historical Formation of the State in Latin America: Some Theoretical and Methodological Guidelines for Its Study." *Latin American Research Review* 16, no. 2 (1981): 3–32.

Padgett, Vincent L. *The Mexican Political System*. Boston: Houghton Mifflin, 1966.

Paz, Octavio. *The Labyrinth of Solitude*. New York: Grove Press, 1961.

Perey, Allison. "The Revolutionary Potential of Mexico in the 1980s." *Journal of International Affairs* 40, no. 2 (1987): 373–85.

Pérez Correa, Fernando. "Contradictions and Continuities in Mexican

Constitutionalism." In *Mexico Today*, edited by Tommie Sue Montgomery, pp. 57–63. Philadelphia: Institute for the Study of Human Issues, 1982.

Peters, John G., and Susan Welch. "Political Corruption in America: Search for Definitions and a Theory or If Political Corruption Is in Mainstream of American Politics, Why Is It Not in Mainstream of American Politics Research." *American Political Science Review* 72 (1978): 974–84.

Pinto-Duschinsky, Michael. "Theories of Corruption in American Politics." Paper presented at the annual meeting of the American Political Science Association, Chicago, 1976.

Poitras, Guy E. "Welfare Bureaucracy and Clientele Politics in Mexico." *Administrative Science Quarterly* 18, no. 1 (1973): 18–26.

"Las principales críticas de Luis J. Garrido en Gobernación, a Gobernación." *Proceso* 642 (February 20, 1989): 30–31.

Presidencia de la República, Unidad de la Crónica Presidencial. *Las razones y las obras: Gobierno de Miguel de la Madrid.* 2 vols. Mexico, 1984, 1985.

Purcell, John F. H., and Susan Kaufman Purcell. "Machine Politics and Socio-Economic Change in Mexico." In *Contemporary Mexico, Papers of the IV International Congress of Mexican History*, edited by James W. Wilkie, Michael C. Meyer, and Edna Monzon de Wilkie, pp. 348–66. Berkeley and Los Angeles: University of California Press, 1976.

Purcell, Susan K. *The Mexican Profit-Sharing Decision: Politics in an Authoritarian Regime.* Berkeley and Los Angeles: University of California Press, 1975.

Purcell, Susan K., and John F. H. Purcell. "The Nature of the Mexican State." Wilson Center Working Papers, no. 1, Washington, D.C.: Wilson Center, 1977.

Quezada, Norberto. "Un modelo del comportamiento corrupto." In *Cinco ensayos sobre la corrupción.* Santiago: Universidad Madre y Maestra, 1980.

Ramírez, Carlos. "Las finanzas de PEMEX a punto de estallar, por corrupción e incapacidad." *Proceso* 238 (May 25, 1981): 6–10.

"Rechazan los priístas que se amplíe la investigación del fraude bursátil." *Proceso* 642 (February 20, 1989): 28–29.

Reisman, W. M. ¿Remedios contra la corrupción? Translated by Mariluz Caso. México: Fondo de Cultura Económica, 1981. Originally published as Folded Lies: Bribery, Crusades and Reforms. New York: Free Press, 1979.

Reyna, José Luis, and Richard S. Weinert, eds. Authoritarianism in Mexico. Philadelphia: Institute for the Study of Human Issues, 1977.

Riding, Alan. Distant Neighbors: A Portrait of the Mexicans. 1984. Reprint. New York: Vintage Books, 1984.

———. "Mexico Police: Symbol of Corruption?" New York Times, February 13, 1983.

Rogow, Arnold, and Harold Lasswell. Power, Corruption and Rectitude. Englewood Cliffs, N.J.: Prentice-Hall, 1963.

Rohter, Larry. "Mexico Taking Bites out of Corruption." Arizona Daily Star, April 19, 1987, p. 7.

———. "Shedding the Losers." Arizona Daily Star, April 19, 1987, p. 5.

Romanucci-Ross, Lola. Conflict, Violence and Morality in a Mexican Village. Palo Alto, Calif.: National Press Books, 1973.

Ronfeldt, David. Atencingo: The Politics of Agrarian Struggle in a Mexican Ejido. Stanford: Stanford University Press, 1973.

Rose-Ackerman, Susan. Corruption: A Study in Political Economy. New York: Academic Press, 1978.

Rosenblaum, Keith. "Wall of Corruption Encircles Sonoran Capital." Arizona Daily Star, August 9, 1987, pp. 1, 4.

Rout, Lawrence. "Mexicans, in Depths of Crisis, Are Irked by Allegations Leaders Spend Lavishly." Wall Street Journal, September 20, 1982, p. 28.

Rubin, Steven M. Mexico: Conditions and Risks for Business. Special Report 1103. London: Economist Intelligence Unit, 1987.

Sanders, Sol. Mexico: Chaos on Our Doorstep. Lanham, Md.: Madison, 1986.

Sanderson, Steven E. "Presidential Succession and Political Rationality in Mexico." World Politics 35 (1983): 315–34.

Secretaría de Gobernación. Renovación moral de la sociedad. México: Talleres Gráficos de la Nación, 1983.

Schneider, Ben Ross. "Partly for Sale: Privatization and State Strength in Brazil and Mexico." *Journal of Interamerican Studies and World Affairs* 30, no. 4 (1988–89): 89–116.

Scott, James C. *Comparative Political Corruption.* Englewood Cliffs, N.J.: Prentice-Hall, 1972.

Scott, Robert E. *Mexican Government in Transition.* Urbana: University of Illinois Press, 1959.

Sherman, Lawrence W. *Scandal and Reform: Controlling Police Corruption.* Berkeley and Los Angeles: University of California Press, 1978.

Sloan, John W. *Public Policy in Latin America: A Comparative Survey.* Pittsburgh: University of Pittsburgh Press, 1984.

Smith, Peter H. *Labyrinths of Power: Political Recruitment in Twentieth-Century Mexico.* Princeton: Princeton University Press, 1979.

————. "Leadership and Change: Intellectuals and Technocrats in Mexico." In *Mexico's Political Stability: The Next Five Years,* edited by Roderic Ai Camp, pp. 101–18. Boulder, Colo.: Westview Press, 1986.

Spalding, Rose. "State Power and Its Limits: Corporatism in Mexico." *Comparative Political Studies* 14 (1981): 139–61.

Stevens, Evelyn P. "Comment: The Mexican Presidential Succession." *Journal of Interamerican Studies and World Affairs* 19, no. 1 (1977): 125–26.

————. "Legality and Extra-Legality in Mexico." *Journal of Interamerican Studies and World Affairs* 12 (1970): 62–75.

————. *Protest and Response in Mexico.* Cambridge, Mass.: MIT Press, 1974.

Stockton, William. "Bribes Are Called a Way of Life for the Mexicans." *New York Times,* October 25, 1986, p. 3.

Story, Dale. "Entrepreneurs and the State in Mexico: Examining the Authoritarian Thesis." Technical Papers Series no. 30. Austin: University of Texas, 1980.

————. *Industry, the State and Public Policy in Mexico.* Austin: University of Texas Press, 1986.

————. "Policy Cycles in Mexican Presidential Politics." *Latin American Research Review* 20 (1985): 139–62.

Street, James H. "Mexico's Development Crisis." *Current History,* March 1987, pp. 101–4, 127–29.

196 / BIBLIOGRAPHY

Tannenbaum, Frank. *Mexico: The Struggle for Peace and Bread.* New York: Knopf, 1950.

Tavares, Flavio. "The Shame of Mexico: Corruption and Mismanagement in a Sea of Oil." *World Press Report* 30 (1983): 26–28.

Tilman, Robert T. "Emergence of Black Market Bureaucracy: Administration, Development and Corruption in the New States." *Public Administration Review* 28 (1968): 440–42. Reprinted in *Political Corruption: Readings and Comparative Analysis,* edited by Arnold J. Heidenheimer, pp. 62–64. New York: Holt, Rinehart and Winston, 1970.

Ugalde, Antonio. *Power and Conflict in a Mexican Community: A Study of Political Integration.* Albuquerque: University of New Mexico Press, 1970.

Vanderwood, Paul J. *Disorder and Progress: Bandits, Police and Mexican Development.* Lincoln: University of Nebraska Press, 1981.

Vera, Jorge Tomás. "Capitalismo y corrupción." *Yucatán: Historia y Economía* 1, no. 4 (1977): 26–52.

Vernon, Raymond. *The Dilemma of Mexico's Development.* Cambridge, Mass.: Harvard University Press, 1963.

Werner, Simcha B. "New Directions in the Study of Administrative Corruption." *Public Administration Review* 43 (1983): 146–54.

Wertheim, Willem F. "Sociological Aspects of Corruption in Southeast Asia." *Sociologica Neerlandica,* 1, no. 2 (Autumn 1963): 129–52. Reprinted in *Political Corruption: Readings and Comparative Analysis,* edited by Arnold J. Heidenheimer, pp. 195–211. New York: Holt, Rinehart and Winston, 1970.

Whitehead, Laurence. "Why Mexico Is Ungovernable—Almost." Working Paper 54. Washington, D.C.: Wilson Center, 1979.

Wiarda, Howard J. "Mexico: The Unraveling of a Corporatist Regime?" *Journal of Interamerican Studies and World Affairs* 30, no. 4 (1988–89): 1–28.

Wilkie, James W. "The Dramatic Growth of Mexico's Economy and the Rise of Statist Government Budgetary Power, 1910–1982." *Mexican Forum* 5, no. 4 (1985): 33–41.

Wilkie, James W., Michael C. Meyer, and Edna Monzon de Wilkie, eds. *Contemporary Mexico: Papers of the IV International Congress of Mexican History.* Berkeley and Los Angeles: University of California Press, 1976.

Wilson, James Q. "Corruption: The Shame of the States." *Public Interest* 2 (1966): 28–38. Reprinted in *Political Corruption: Readings and Comparative Analysis,* edited by Arnold J. Heidenheimer, pp. 298–306. New York: Holt, Rinehart and Winston, 1970.

Wolf, Eric. *Sons of the Shaking Earth.* Chicago: University of Chicago Press, 1959.

Wraith, Ronald E., and Edgar Simpkins. *Corruption in Developing Countries.* London: Allen & Unwin, 1963.

Wyman, Donald L. *Mexico's Economic Crisis: Challenges and Opportunities.* Monograph Series, 12. San Diego: Center for U.S.-Mexican Studies, University of California, 1983.

Zeitlin, Maurice. *Revolutionary Politics and the Cuban Working Class.* Princeton: Princeton University Press, 1970.

Newspapers and News Periodicals

Arizona Daily Star (Tucson); *Arizona Republic* (Phoenix); *Christian Science Monitor; El Día* (Mexico City); *Excélsior* (Mexico City); *El Heraldo* (Mexico City); *Información Sistemática* (Mexico City); *Mexico City News; Mexico Journal* (Mexico City); *Mexico Today* (Mexico City); *El Nacional* (Mexico City); *New York Times; Novedades* (Mexico City); *Ovaciones* (Mexico City); *La Prensa* (Mexico City); *Proceso* (Mexico City); *El Sol* (Mexico City); *Tiempo* (Mexico); *Tucson Citizen; Universal* (Mexico City); *Unomasuno* (Mexico City); *Vuelta* (Mexico); and *Washington Post.*

Index

Forrest Colburn, "Mexico's
Financial Crisis"
Latin American Research
Review 1984 or 1985

George Grayson